T0128477

MILLENNIAL KINGDOM ENTREPRENEUR

ODELL PALACIO

WESTBOW
PRESS®
A DIVISION OF THOMAS NELSON
& ZONDERVAN

Copyright © 2018 Odell Palacio.

Book cover design: Immar Palomera
Editorial direction: Jonah Mixon-Webster

All rights reserved. No part of this book may be used or reproduced by any means, graphic, electronic, or mechanical, including photocopying, recording, taping or by any information storage retrieval system without the written permission of the author except in the case of brief quotations embodied in critical articles and reviews.

This book is a work of non-fiction. Unless otherwise noted, the author and the publisher make no explicit guarantees as to the accuracy of the information contained in this book and in some cases, names of people and places have been altered to protect their privacy.

WestBow Press books may be ordered through booksellers or by contacting:

WestBow Press
A Division of Thomas Nelson & Zondervan
1663 Liberty Drive
Bloomington, IN 47403
www.westbowpress.com
1 (866) 928-1240

Because of the dynamic nature of the Internet, any web addresses or links contained in this book may have changed since publication and may no longer be valid. The views expressed in this work are solely those of the author and do not necessarily reflect the views of the publisher, and the publisher hereby disclaims any responsibility for them.

Any people depicted in stock imagery provided by Getty Images are models, and such images are being used for illustrative purposes only. Certain stock imagery © Getty Images.

ISBN: 978-1-9736-4684-6 (sc)
ISBN: 978-1-9736-4685-3 (hc)
ISBN: 978-1-9736-4683-9 (e)

Library of Congress Control Number: 2018914082

Print information available on the last page.

WestBow Press rev. date: 12/6/2018

Scripture quotations marked AMPC are taken from the
Amplified® Bible, Copyright © 1954, 1958, 1962, 1964, 1965,
1987 by The Lockman Foundation. Used by permission.

Scripture quotations marked CEV are taken from the Contemporary English
Version®, Copyright © 1995 American Bible Society. All rights reserved.

Scripture quotations marked ESV are taken from The ESV® Bible (The Holy
Bible, English Standard Version®). ESV® Text Edition: 2016. Copyright © 2001
by Crossway, a publishing ministry of Good News Publishers. All rights reserved.

Scripture quotations marked KJV are taken from the King
James Version of the Bible. Public domain.

Scripture quotations marked MSG are taken from The Message.
Copyright © 1993, 1994, 1995, 1996, 2000, 2001, 2002.
Used by permission of NavPress Publishing Group.

Scripture quotations marked NIV are taken from The Holy Bible, New
International Version®, NIV® Copyright © 1973, 1978, 1984, 2011 by
Biblica, Inc.® Used by permission. All rights reserved worldwide.

Scripture quotations marked NIRV taken from the Holy Bible, New
International Reader's Version®. Copyright © 1996, 1998 Biblica. All
rights reserved throughout the world. Used by permission of Biblica.

Scripture quotations marked NKJV are taken from the New King James Version®.
Copyright © 1982 by Thomas Nelson. Used by permission. All rights reserved.

Scripture quotations marked NLT are taken from the Holy Bible,
New Living Translation, copyright © 1996, 2004, 2015 by Tyndale
House Foundation. Used by permission of Tyndale House Publishers,
Inc., Carol Stream, Illinois 60188. All rights reserved.

CONTENTS

To Jesus - Thank You.

To my wife and children,
for your patience as we experienced the lessons
that made the contents of this book.
We're on our way.

INTRODUCTION

It has taken time for me to understand the biblical perspective of entrepreneurship and the difference in application of this perspective between western and eastern cultures. There are families who thrive, generationally, through economic preservation, entrepreneurship and community development while many other families have adopted the false sense of security by going to school to get a job and promoting oneself to be an asset to a company (rather than to their community). What I learned influenced the creation of this book—it was never God's intention for an individual to not thrive in their area of gifting. Instead, God's desire is for us to influence and excel.

A few factors stood out: age is a made-up prerequisite, entrepreneurship is not a young person's sport, it's an ambitious person's sport. As a matter of fact, many great businesses were started by older entrepreneurs. Albeit, when younger, one can take more risk and find funding through crowdfunding platforms or elevator pitch / business plan writing grant competitions. Some older entrepreneurs are more conservative and fund through 401Ks, their 403b, or Home Equity Lines of Credit. Regardless of age, knowing how to apply your gift leveraging today's technology and resources is progressive. Lastly, time and information are you best assets. I was also able to identify two distinct personality traits of the entrepreneur—the chaser and the runner. Allow me to ask a few questions, would you follow a quitter? Also, is it easier to follow someone focused on one thing or someone trying to accomplish several things at once? Lastly, would you expect someone to follow you if you haven't pushed yourself and fought for your dream? Commitment shows passion and a desire to accomplish - it is very necessary to have commitment in your heart because commitment is character! Through commitment you learn the lesson from each test with a surety to not repeat the same mistakes. Inconsistency in your commitment results in a continual delay of your goals. A chaser is committed throughout the journey, a runner is committed throughout the emotion and excitement.

This book is also a diary of sorts. I've failed a million times but keep getting back up. My inspiration to write this book is to encourage entrepreneurs worldwide with the Word of God, to illustrate the direct correlation about the vision, the words you choose, and the course of action you take. Are you a chaser or a runner? Entrepreneurship is not a fairytale, there are hills and valley. Spotting opportunity, staying motivated, having a willingness to learn, and maximizing your time are lessons that you will acquire throughout your process.

I'll never encourage someone to leave their job, but I do encourage you to use your God given talents to take appropriate risks in business. Some "entrepreneurs" are best suited for a number two position and do not want the responsibility of leading, instead they prefer to add value. When these people are in the correct environment, they can use their God given entrepreneurial gifts to help the company. Again, there's an entrepreneur in all of us, the key is to be faithful to your call.

Faithfulness is an attribute of character, faithfulness in commitment leads to tangible manifestation. Faithfulness can be synonymous with loyalty and allows the faithful person to believe in the dream when they stand alone.

In Hebrew, the word faithful is synonymous with the word firm, this same word is the root for the words Amen and true. Thus, to be faithful regarding your dream means you're being firm, staying true to it and you're coming into agreement with God by saying "so be it." Faith is very important in the Kingdom. Faith replaces your five senses and is also the currency of the Kingdom. Live what you see with your imagination and be firm in its pursuit. Understand that the Kingdom you represent is progressive, faith encourages progression.

Entrepreneurship is a spiritual journey that requires a firm and definite decision. In Luke 9:62 NIRV Jesus teaches us to stay firm in our decision making saying, "Suppose you start to plow and then look back. If you do, you are not fit for service in God's kingdom." We can understand this to mean "a double-minded man, unstable in all his ways" James 1:8 ESV, be firm, be faithful.

The foundation of the book is from 2 Kings 4:1-7 NIV, a story I've heard preached several times with each rendition offering similar insight, but it is a most appropriate scripture for this text because the bible declares that God is the same yesterday, today, and forever. This excerpt provides a great example of entrepreneurship for generations to come. Another reason I admire this particular passage is because I come from a single-parent (mother) household where my mother was an entrepreneur and lunch lady who came to América from Panamá raising her two children alone (after my parents divorced), and I can testify that "I've never seen the godly abandoned or their children begging for bread." - Psalms 37:25 NLT

You (and I) were never created to just live the life that was handed to us - matter of fact I believe we were created for entrepreneurship which requires knowing your oil, cultivating your oil, and allowing time and culture to prove its authenticity. It is my belief, and the sentiment of this book, that not all entrepreneurs are successful, only the ones who press their unique oil (not the oil everyone seems to be sharing), know how to spot opportunities, and are patient while maximizing opportunities, will see success through entrepreneurship. The life of an effective entrepreneur has its turns, potholes and abrupt stops (in which a chaser will turn into inspiration, while a runner will use as a means to abandon).

I define entrepreneurship as *"the management up until [and afterwards] manifestation of an idea that becomes profitable and produces wealth."* Business News Daily defines entrepreneurship as *"the development of a business from the ground up — coming up with an idea and turning it into a profitable business."*

I believe God created humans with the ability to use gifts and resources (in collaboration with God) to work Eden. The basis for this thesis is found in Genesis 1:28-30 NKJV, Genesis 2:15-16 NKJV, and Deuteronomy 8:18 NKJV. My belief is that God made us in his image and commanded us to have dominion, to use our creativity to create opportunities and wealth (but creativity must be unlocked). So, the entrepreneur can influence culture and expand the Kingdom of God, because *business is ministry, and ministry is business.* When God told Adam to "be fruitful and multiply," I believe the Lord was saying "bring forth and excel" then God gave Adam more instructions, "have dominion and subdue," meaning, "prevail against and bring into subjection" all things you have access to. In other words, "I've given you all you need to be successful, prevail against the things you don't understand, bring those into your order. You must 'avodah' to excel." See, God created Adam because God had no one to manage the Earth God created - therefore, everything on Earth, although it belongs to God is for us to manage, use, learn more about, and excel in for our particular area of gifting. Everything Adam needed he already had access to—everything you have access to can be used to help you thrive. Read that part again and highlight it! You have the ability to create wealth (and most importantly) establish (and expand) His Kingdom once you learn to become who God intended for you to become and realize all the tools you need are right in front of you.

So what's avodah? Avodah is the Hebrew word for work, worship, and service. It is used interchangeably throughout the Old Testament, it is used in Genesis 2:15-God took the Man and set him down in the Garden of Eden to work (avodah) the ground and keep it in order. I find this interesting, Adam embodied the entire translation of avodah - his work was worship to God, service to God and his help, and was general work as well. How did God reward Adam? Through bringing him help and unlocking creativity, in Genesis 2:18-19 ESV—The Lord God said, "It is not good for the man to be alone. I will make a helper who is just right for him."

Now out of the ground the Lord God formed every beast of the field and every bird of the heavens and brought them to man to see what he would call them. Whatever word the man called each creature, that word became the creature's name.

If you're struggling with entrepreneurship and you're saying, "I'm working hard and serving others," my question is, "are you worshipping?" Worship is the attribute of avodah that brings revelation (and when you're fully in avodah you unlock creativity). My other question will also be, are you performing in your purpose or are you attempting to thrive using someone else's oil?

Adam knew why he was created and was successful in that because he was constant in avodah (in its entirety). Stop pressing an oil you have no business working. You may be serving people in the wrong area (or with the wrong heart)? Or you're using the image of entrepreneurship as means to seek worship (and praise) for yourself?

A few years back, while taking my undergraduate studies during our Race and Ethics lecture, our professor asked, "Is there such thing as a ghetto?" Physically, of course - I replied, then a peer (wasn't even a classmate - was there visiting the professor) responded and said "no, there isn't it's all mental." I did not and still do not agree with his position but as time went on I realized something, he confused "ghetto" with "poverty consciousness." Read the book of Exodus, it will literally blow your mind. God delivered Israel from Egypt, every family prosperous. In the wilderness, for 40 years - their shoes and clothing never had a hole, God sent bread from heaven, meat (qual), and water from a rock. Yet they were mentally stuck in Egypt. See, something in our subconscious accepts failure as norm and poverty as holy. Thus, everything (including your business) is stuck in a paradigm that supports you not being fruitful.

I am originally from Panama - migrating to America, "the promised land." meant there were/are no limits. So, why did I place them on myself and my business? The American dream is to receive education that will be suitable for the growth of your God given talent! God's words do not return unto Him void and anything He's told you can be done. Yes, there will be days you want to give up and yes there will be (for some), sleepless nights, and others cycles where you work on the idea till you burn out then take a week off till inspiration hits you, but all in all, this book is written to get you the information you need to be your potential.

"The impact of the entrepreneur is transcultural; business funds influence, grows economies, and develops communities. Most importantly, Kingdom entrepreneurs fund the expansion of the Kingdom of God."

—Odell Palacio

CHAPTER 1

Different Types of Millennials and Their Oil

1 The wife of a man from the company of the prophets cried out to Elisha, "Your servant my husband is dead, and you know that he revered the Lord. But now his creditor is coming to take my two boys as his slaves."

2 Elisha replied to her, "How can I help you? Tell me, what do you have in your house?"

"Your servant has nothing there at all," she said, "except a **small jar of olive oil.***"*

3 Elisha said, "Go around and ask all your neighbors for empty jars. Don't ask for just a few.

4 Then go inside and shut the door behind you and your sons. Pour oil into all the jars, and as each is filled, put it to one side."

5 She left him and shut the door behind her and her sons. They brought the jars to her and she kept pouring.

> *6 When all the jars were full, she said to her*
> *son, "Bring me another one."*
>
> *But he replied, "There is not a jar left." Then the oil stopped flowing.*
>
> *7 She went and told the man of God, and he said, "Go, sell the oil*
> *and pay your debts. You and your sons can live on what is left."*
>
> *2 Kings 4:1-7 NIV*

The Bible is filled with instructional narratives that can assist you in your walk as you navigate through obstacles or adjust to successes, Reading the Bible helps me keep God's words in my heart to coach myself by what God says verses by what I feel or see. Oftentimes, I find myself combating against walking by faith while dealing with reality. For entrepreneurs, faith confronts our realities by providing an alternative to our five senses which create our insecurities. Faith is our imagination in our work.

Your oil challenges the stronghold of lack and worry; your oil is the antidote to your inability to produce. *2 Kings Chapter 4 verses 1 - 7 NIV* speaks loudly to me about entrepreneurship, it is the building block of this book and the reference point to encourage, develop, inspire or guide entrepreneurs but we must dissect it to discover the principles of entrepreneurship that God was revealing to us. There's a widow (newer) with debts (a lot) and children (two sons and a shortage of money to provide for all expenses.)

Everyone's life is different, you may not be a widow, but you may be recently divorced, newly married or a high school graduate that doesn't want to go to college. Maybe you're a college graduate looking for a job paying a salary enough to afford rent downtown Ann Arbor, a single parent, high school dropout, the standout employee rising the ranks quickly, or the youngest CEO in the history of the Fortune 500

Company you work for. I want you to take whatever situation you're in and place yourself in the widow's shoes. Class or status does not matter when life happens, I believe that we all face a moment in life where we have to determine the magnitude of the fight in us to navigate towards our goal. The widow had to adjust to life without a crutch-let me explain, the widow and now single mother, was operating under her husband's anointing for so long she forgot hers, in other words; once she got married and had someone else to lean on, she let her talent rest and did not tap into her gifts because her husband's gifts were sufficient to pay the bills, put food in the fridge, and take care of the needs of their children. Much like the widow, as you commence the journey of entrepreneurship you'll have a face to face with your potential while you adjust to life without your crutch - now he's gone and she must stand on her own, relearn her gift and walk in its anointing or become a beggar going from person to person to ask for help.

Entrepreneurship is birthed by way of two mediums, either path leading to solving a problem which bring gratification to your customer- the identification of a vacancy in the marketplace and a whisper in your heart that directs in dealing with a life changing moment which requires adjustments at home. Regardless of what category you find yourself in as you begin your entrepreneurship journey, at one point on this journey you'll have to acknowledge and eliminate your crutch! Full disclaimer, writing this first chapter (and revisiting the start of my journey) taught me a lot about myself and my own process (no two stories are entirely alike but there are common scenarios in each entrepreneurial journey). This reality check is gut wrenching, Elisha was forcing a mind adjustment in midst of tragedy but implying that she cannot coast through life dependent on others while feeling entitled to their support - blaze a new trail and thrive.

In the reference excerpt, oil means anointing, the Man of God asked her, "what do you have in your house," she responds, "just a pot of oil." Allow me to translate, the Man of God asked, "what do you have that we can work with?" She responds, "well I got this talent tucked away, I rarely use it." The Bible declares in Deuteronomy 8:18 CEV "instead, remember that the LORD your God gives you the strength to make a living. That's how he keeps the promise he made to your ancestors." Do you know that you have a tailored made talent or gift, that if cultivated, the strength you need to make a living will flow out from it which will give you the ability to create wealth and be a culture influencer but your crutch, your need for validation, and your comparisons to others, keeps you from cultivating the one thing that can guide you through your entrepreneurial quest towards your destiny.

When you research to define the word anoint, it means to *nominate or choose (someone) as successor to or leading candidate for a position.* When you recognize what you have and you cultivate it, you open the door to allow yourself to lead that industry or influence a new trend! All of this from **2 Kings 4:1-7 NIV**? Yes, but wait! There's more... Elisha was telling this woman, I can't give you anything outside of what you already have. You don't lack anything, you just haven't tapped into yourself yet. In Luke 6:38 CEV Jesus tells us that If you give to others, you will be given a full amount in return. It will be packed down, shaken together, and spilling over into your lap. Jesus taught us to serve others, how do we serve? Well, there are several ways but, in this book, and this chapter we'll focus on service through the anointing on our gift(s)!

This single mother forgot her talents or never cultivated them because she was in a situation that allowed her to table her gifts and leave them (for a season) without nurturing them. Much like yourself; the widow was an entrepreneur with untapped potential - she housed a unique gift but was trying to fit in a world by following its rules and patterns instead of cultivating and tapping into her purpose. We know these rules because they're in our lives today, go to college, get a house with a picket fence, a good job, get married, have two kids and get a dog. These are the rules that govern your life, they are the barometer by which you follow but these rules aren't fair for all players dependent on where you're from, the color of your skin, sexual preference, and religion. These rules aren't meant for you to prosper or thrive, they are meant for you to become robots and die. She was a robot coasting, governed by rules that don't tell her how to adjust to tragedy than Elisha says, activate what's been dormant - change your limits, tap into the anointing God has given you because the gifts and calling of God are without repentance. - Romans 11:29 KJV

I love how the Man of God handled this, the widow, instead of receiving what she expected to receive from the Man of God, which was a handout. She was met with, "go, become!" It's funny because I've encountered people who, unaware of their own oil, position their interactions from a sense of entitlement, much like the widow has; "you know my husband, he went to your school - you know he feared God and served you... you owe me!" Plato is recorded as saying "the beginning is the most important part of the work." I believe he was saying - the hardest part isn't learning what you're destined to become, the hardest part is taking the first step.

Influence by Your Own Oil

I love to cook and create but my favorite thing to do is bake. I like making the entire meal from start to finish; thus, I think I perfected the lost art of cooking good homemade meals and being able to feed a family which everyone is full and satisfied. This passion of mine extends to my competitive side, I'll go to a restaurant then come home and try to recreate that recipe again, especially the deserts. Why am I bringing this up? Well, honestly this book is inspired by my story of owning my marketing agency and the challenges I had to overcome, each step documented. Consider this as my private journal now open to the public. Everything has been something personally done or learned along the way, the opportunities I learned from and the maturation necessary to achieve. God rewards when you have the capacity to handle, I've constantly had to encourage myself, daily! I wanted to document my story in hopes of encouraging and uplifting other entrepreneurs along their way, I believe it is very important to share the story which is between idea and success because the beauty of entrepreneurship is the ability to persevere there isn't a cookie cutter approach to entrepreneurship. Much like boxing, you can't play entrepreneur. Approach your anointing with faith and powered by commitment.

So what was my oil? Art! Not just any art. I love Mola. I grew up in a Panamanian household and my wife is from Honduras (so I eat and learn a lot about Honduran art and culture). I jumped into art through food-October 3rd, 2012 and named it P'Lacio's, we catered (out of our home) specializing in Panamanian and Honduran street foods (which is full with so much color and love). My culinary experience began with Italian cuisine - since my Junior year of high school (late 1999) till 2009 (when I graduated College) I worked at an Italian restaurant, every role except bartending, so I had a lot of experience with food and hospitality but P'Lacio's was a vacancy that I found an opportunity to fill. It allowed me to leverage experience with passion (art) and I heard this quiet peaceful voice encouraging me to pursue.

Before you start to think that once you identify your gift it's on like Donkey Kong, you're wrong-there's a fight to grow and cultivate, perfect then implement. I had such a strong conviction with this dream that I quit my job-which paid very well-to work full time on P'Lacio's (10/31/2012).

My kitchen; the refrigerator, the stove, oven and ingredients are my tools, remember there was the oil (or anointing) then there were the pots. What's your tools? For you, it may be a computer, phone, a car or truck, lawnmower, paper and pencils, a sewing machine, a comb, or perhaps you want to design a woman's cosmetic line (oils) or you're great with numbers (a calculator), it is important to identify your tools because every anointing has tools! This pot of oil is special, often times we store our anointing away, the irony is we know where it's at we just never thought of using it to serve others. It's like asking a person who is great at working on cars where his tools are, he'll say "the garage" but he wouldn't consider that he could have a great side hustle or a booming business if those 'once in a while' tools became used for everyday purpose. God provides us each with the tools and resources we need to dominate in our areas of gifting and make an impact, what we do with those tools are totally up to us.

God blessed Noah and his sons and said to them "be fruitful and multiply" in the book of Genesis chapter 9 verse 7. But if you read verses 1 - 6 you'll see prior to the command of multiplication God established a covenant of dominion on everything on the Earth except for killing another man. Here's what that means, once you identify your idea, or position yourself (which is your advantage - given to you by your Maker) and you're in pursuit (of becoming your potential) everything around you will work out for the good and for your use, they become your tools. At one point, Noah and his family (wife, three sons and their wives, plus a few animals) were the only people on the Earth, I believe the "be fruitful and multiply" command included more than only producing children. For example, Noah was a gardener, the soil was his oil - he made vineyards (used tools) which produced crops and wine (his business), the woman Elisha spoke with used pots to house her anointing and I use my kitchen. What are the tools laying around the house that you have access to, the ones you use when working on your passion? Identification produces the product the market is waiting for!

Understanding the Seed

In every seed is the potential of a garden, orchard, or forest. Look again at the response from Elisha; "How can I help you? Tell me, what do you have in your house?" Elisha offers assistance and a solution.

A seed has two possible uses; one can spend it, or one can plant it. I have mistakenly used seeds through spending, but once the process is understood it becomes obvious that growth is the path desired. Let me explain these seeds as money, let's say I give you $200 USD and say, "go get licensed to start your business," let's assume you and the widow have common circumstances you're facing. To use by spending will be to use the $200 to pay a bill—you'll justify it by saying "that's the responsible thing to do." Now that $200 was brought to use by spending. To use the seed by planting will be to take that same $200 and invest it in to your business. Perhaps you want to be a real estate agent but need the money to accomplish your required training, you invest (or plant) the seed so it can produce an orchard.

Seeds in entrepreneurship are path altering, imagine you are given a watermelon whose seeds you decide to wait (or the spring to plant instead of roasting and eating, in turn you can produce watermelon to sell. This is what Elisha did here, he taught the woman to view her oil (anointing) as a producer of wealth that can reach maturity once cultivated (poured out / used), packaged (go to your neighbors and ask for bottles), then distributed.

As a young man I thought seeds were matured at consumption, I didn't understand agriculture. I didn't grow up with an alternative point of view which would serve as compasses to guide wealth building and drive business development. So my friends and I would get money have great ideas, but wouldn't put them to use because we were trained to mature through consumption by watching our families living paycheck to paycheck or in debt just to give us everything they never had (see how crazy that sounds?) When I understood and applied the principle of agriculture in entrepreneurship and finances, I recognized the package of a seed should not influence my approach towards its handle and care. In some instances, a seed is money, others it's a new job or opportunity (where you start as a temp), in some cases it is a word of knowledge! All three of these packages have the potential to produce a harvest for you, solely dependent upon the handle and care (management) of the money, opportunity, or information.

The woman in our text had an option to listen and ignore or listen and apply. Her response illustrated that she was at a point of no longer obtaining a willingness to tolerate poverty - thus all she needed to do is adhere to the rules. Are there any seeds that you may have mismanaged? The key is not to dwell there but to become aware of the opportunities when they circle back. Entrepreneurs must be alert and aware so they can guide their seed and it can produce. As an entrepreneur, you're a farmer, cultivation is key for the growth of your seed (oil / anointing).

Your "Why"

Motivational speaker Eric Thomas asked the crowd in attendance during one of his speaking engagements I attended at Eastern Michigan University, "What's your 'why?" A simple question with such a moving meaning. So you know what you want to do, you've identified your tools but what drives you to accomplish your goal? This is important because you're going to have days, weeks (and for some) months and years where you're questioning if your business idea is good, you're going to have moments where you'll be talked about and ridiculed, but what's your "why?"

This text is important because the widow's desperation created a supernatural level of faith that she never experienced. But the Man of God's response activated the change. What if I were to tell you that pain has birthed some of the greatest ideas ever, would you believe me? What if I were to say that entrepreneurship can come from a place inspired by the need for change, would you believe me? But, what if I were to tell you that those two are not enough, would you still believe me?

In dissecting the text, we learn the widow is familiar with Elisha, according to the NIV text, the widow's husband was *from the company of the prophets.* So she was familiar with seeing amazing things happen and hearing prophecies and some part of her felt that the "company of Prophets" abandoned her and her family in their time of need, otherwise, what gives her the audacity to remind Elisha that her husband was a follower, servant, and student? To me, Elisha's response should have crushed her and would have for some of you reading this! He didn't give her access to a bridge card (which I once had), he didn't bring her food (which people have helped me with) nor did he send her money (which has happened to me also), no he said, "Get busy, God will bless you!" His instruction made her a top oil saleswoman in her region, but it required her "why" which was at a level of "I cannot lose my children continuing to be lazy" miracle level. The widow received a "this will be a process miracle, not an overnight success story." She couldn't have had a better response! I too had to learn how to get off my butt and partner my dreams with work ethic, in return we no longer ask for handouts, instead we've been gifted with the ability to give!

The "why' is a concoction of desperation and faith (imagination) mixed with a splash of purpose and passion on the rocks. In the New Testament we see a similar level of fire when the women with the issue of blood pushed through a crowd saying to herself "if I can just touch the hem of his garment," what was her why? To be considered clean and normal after years of loneliness and separation (being considered unclean - see Leviticus 15:19-33 NKJV). Her response from God was suddenly because she overcame the process of the push; "at just the right time we will reap a harvest of blessing if we don't give up." - Galatians 6:9 NLT

Until you have a reason motivating you to succeed your idea will remain an idea, not a profitable business model. Whatever success is defined as by you there must be a reason to get to it, a push that's uncomfortable yet worth it!

Missing the Mark

My wife has a unique perspective about the reference verse, her insight was unique to how the verse spoke to her but very relevant in the formation of this subtopic. My wife's point of view is that, the husband was exposed to a way of living that encouraged proper management; financial, physical, and spiritual. His mismanagement lead to the family being buried in debt and yet it was his death that lead to the family thriving. There was a major error here by the husband; he had access to a wealth of knowledge but didn't properly apply what he learned. Sometimes you can be so close to something and still not see it. The wife - who in her submission to her husband, stopped using her gift. Brother's listen, sometimes our wives have the answers but you're so busy trying to lead, you lead your family in the wrong direction - while having access to the right information.

Action

I toyed with naming this book "The Imaginary Line of Entrepreneurship," the idea behind the title was the distinguishing between the entrepreneur and the dreamer. This imaginary line is called "action." You're a creative being made in an image and likeness of God, this is established in Genesis chapters 1 and 2 but in John chapter 1 NKJV we learn that in the beginning was the Word, and the Word was with God, and the Word was God. *2 He was in the beginning with God. 3 All things were made through him, and without him was not anything made that was made.* The word "word" can be understood as an "expression of a thought, in other words it was an idea - spoken aloud (action). We miss this, we miss the power of action. You cannot be comfortable simply in knowing you are made in God's image and likeness if you don't do as God has done and act, like the husband, some of us know too much but do so little. The fail of potential is the inability to be active, unquestionably; your accountability to what you gift the world is based on what you're willing to give of yourself.

Patience

In this chapter I introduce a concept which classifies two sets of entrepreneurs. In my experience, everyone is born with this creative pulse that is reflective of the God which made you. This creative pulse is there to give you a spiritual desire and direct you towards your purpose. The difference is the action and patience. Patience is the ability to accept or tolerate delay while holding on to your promise. Patience is a learned trait; the bible tells us in Psalm 37:7 NIV to "Be still before the Lord and wait patiently for him; do not fret when people succeed in their ways." Caleb, Abraham, and David all waited but the key is to be proactive while waiting. Entrepreneurs that know their oil must be willing to wait its course otherwise something will present itself simpler, perhaps more attractive and (potentially) more lucrative (at the moment) to entice you to abandon the promised route of process through action to what seems easier. You cannot be responsible for the pressing of someone else's oil. You have to work your own oil. Proverbs 16:32 NIV reads "Better a patient person than a warrior, one with self-control than one who takes a city." Patience prepares you for a victorious finish, it allows you to plan all the way to the end. The patient entrepreneur is a chaser; they approach their gift as a benefit to the world. Although the pursuit is a self-sought ambition, the end product has the potential to impact more people than they personally know.

Chasers vs. Runners

This concept is not only unique to my experience, God revealed it to me after my frustration in the [unsuccessful] attempt to open the restaurant (P'Lacio's), initially. Many ideas were birthed during this season, due in part to, my lack of patience and persistence. I think God gave me an eye opener and brought forth the concept once, in the area I lived in, a few restaurant concepts started opening serving Guatemalan food or offering menu items from different regions of Central America. Additionally, I noticed some colleagues of mine from church sticking with a plan and seeing it through, some in hair and makeup, and others in residential cleaning and landscaping.

What I would do is say to myself, "This is taking too long, I'll sell real estate since I can't find a building for P'Lacio's. I'll learn how selling commercial and residential properties works." Then I would say, "Since I can't afford for someone to design the menu and artwork for P'Lacio's or any marketing material for real estate, I'll get trained and certified in digital marketing and learn Adobe Photoshop and Canva and market my creativity." See, all these concepts were to come eventually but I was supposed to build foundation with deep roots before branching out! I was a runner, I sought quick results as affirmation (or validation) that I was, in fact, doing something and that I was talented. It was like I was fighting against naysayers that only existed in my own mind—I wanted to birth my ideas in the universe but what I had to learn, quickly, is that true success is in educating, perfecting, and persevering which is called "establishing the foundation."

It's advantageous to have a blueprint for your life, like most architects, it guides you along the way, but you can only build as high as your foundation will support. The weight of glory is heavy, you don't want to crumble because you didn't strengthen and equip your foundation that allows you to carry weight! The chaser sees entrepreneurship as a marathon, they don't assume they can go 26 miles and 385 yards without proper training (foundation). The chaser is patient and persistent, they focus on passing the current level before worrying about the next and they aren't easily detoured, they explore their other ideas (or ventures) once their primary idea (foundation) is strong enough to carry the weight. Additionally, in the chaser's patience, they understand that moving too fast an entrepreneur might miss their potential target. The objective is to perfect your business through each phase of your process. A lot of people I've encountered maintained a philosophy that entrepreneurship is performing several ideas at once, we watch TV and see celebrities with various means of income, so we emulate, but chasers realize that there is a root before there are branches. Steve Harvey is someone I admire greatly, but before there was Steve Harvey the Author, Talk Show host, Game Show host, Radio Host, Investor and entrepreneur, there was Steve Harvey the comedian. Own and perfect your level, your [perfected] gift will place you before kings. This is the chasers approach.

Chasers are on a journey towards their original state. Entrepreneurship is your original state of dominion which (potentially) leads to royalty and stateliness—therefore entrepreneurs are admired, even those broke ones who take great Instagram pictures, why? It is associated with greatness and everyone watching acknowledges that entrepreneurship is something to strive towards. But to become royal and stately, the prerequisite is called hard work. God told Adam in Genesis 3:17 ESV "Because you have listened to the voice of your wife and have eaten of the tree of which I commanded you, 'You shall not eat of it,' cursed is the ground because of you; in pain you shall eat of it all the days of your life." This means that the very nature of entrepreneurship will require strength and courage because the enemy doesn't want you finding yourself and defining your purpose, and you must push past the barriers. At one point, Adam had it good and without toil but since the Fall, the advantage of abundance came with the requirement of work, it will take more of us to obtain our natural state. Hard work has been like a curse but it's really the ability to use your mind efficiently and effectively; being attentive to direction, leveraging relationships and employing those smarter than you. Strength and courage lead to royalty and stateliness for entrepreneurs. Successful entrepreneurs (chasers) are esteemed highly and become the barometer of an industry while the runners become lessons of what not to do. Jesus came to restore what Adam lost, imagine embracing the Kingdom of God while cultivating your unique gift—you'll start to walk in your own lane.

Remember the widow? She went to the Man of God for a quick fix experience and was forced to be a chaser, to be patience and see everything through. Choosing entrepreneurship is to think long term— cultivating your gift is like shining and taking care of the pot the oil is held in. The chaser concept simply states; time invested chasing the development of your gift is never wasted but is an investment towards the state of your future. The chaser's friends are like-minded, s/he seeks education to perfect their craft, s/he plans with the end in mind and isn't easily influenced by the emotion of excitement, the chaser is a calculated aggressive whose intent supports the goal. The runner approach is vastly different, where the urgency to destiny negatively impacts the effect of your purpose; they are haste and impatient, they abandon ideas before planting in good soil because they want the end by forsaking the process. Proverbs 19:2 NIV says, "Desire without knowledge is not good—how much more will hasty feet miss the way!"

In my experience, it isn't ideal to say you're an entrepreneur without a solid foundation; otherwise, you're an unstable individual who won't allow for themselves to grow a concept till it reaches success or exhaust its potential. Runners are naturals at entrepreneurship but are impatient, they want things to happen overnight or want money fast. As far as I can remember I was selling and employing, I would buy candy from Sam's club and sell it on the bus for a buck or get a paper route and hire my friends to deliver the papers but my environment encouraged a money fast approach—not until I met my mentor did I learn the long way is the correct way.

In this first chapter I wanted to help you identify your anointing and your toots and learn your "why." Lastly, I wanted to remind you of the process. Take some time to write these things down:

1. What are you good at that comes natural to you?
2. What are the tools you already have access to that can help you perfect your gift?
3. What is your "why?"

4. Write down your goals and give the goal a date; then work backward.

Lesson 1: Your pot of oil is your gift, start cultivating your gift to be an effective millennial entrepreneur. Entrepreneurs match their gifts to the people who need them.

CHAPTER 2

Mastery is Maturity: Learn Before You Earn

Learning is so important to me; I try to read and/or listen to +20 business books annually. These books usually focus on leadership, economics, trade, marketing, business motivation, market research, discipline, and other topics. My personal mission statement is, "To be a blessing to others." Every project I work on falls under this mission, as does everything I learn—learning helps me better my approach towards my mission.

To become a resourceful blessing, I believe I have to become a master of something and not a jack of all trades. Education makes you a master. I love the study the transliteration of light and darkness in the bible. Light translates to knowledge, while darkness translates to ignorance—to God, we should be hungry for knowledge by chasing the kingdom and perfecting our gifts. As a matter of fact, it's an injustice to have a gift and stay ignorant because we will be held accountable for how we use our gifts and our time.

Average people approach their gift with average ambition. If you just do a bit extra you become celebrated—and therefore learning before earning is leverage. You have a great idea, and of course you know it will work. Think of your "If I can just get a chance..." speech that you've practiced on your friends and family a million times. Have you first considered perfecting your craft and finding an accountability partner or a mentor?

Information is acquired through self-study or inheritance, having mentors can help you learn, help you identify your areas of opportunity, and help you maximize the potential of your business and your time. I learned the concept of mentorship to be the preferred maximizer of time. A mentor, most often than not, is willing to invest their time to ensure that you do not make costly mistakes and that your road to success is simpler to navigate. You must be willing to allow someone to look at your plans without prejudice and with a clean perspective. This person will guide you to profit and see success. A really good mentor also has a mentor, they are being held accountable as well. That's the key. Never become too large in your own mind to think that you are unable to receive growth strategies or practices that will better your endeavors.

The fastest way from point A to point B is not a straight line, yet it's hardly ever that simple. For you, the fastest way from point A to point B is mastery and mentorship. To master, you must forget all you know and really decide to learn and commit to continual learning. The mentor then comes in and throws a curveball which feels like it's pulling you further away from the goal but really the curve becomes a force that pulls you closer to your goal.

Google defines mentorship as "*a relationship in which a more experienced or more knowledgeable person helps to guide a less experienced or less knowledgeable person.* Based on personal experience I've defined mentorship as *someone who is invested in your success professionally, providing lessons from their mistakes which direct you towards your potential.*" The Bible declares in James 1:5 ESV, "If any of you lack wisdom, let him ask God, who gives generously to all without reproach, and it will be given him." One way to attain wisdom [from God] is borrowed from a direct (or indirect) mentor that feels appointed by the Holy Spirit. An indirect mentor is an author or speaker that God has pressed in your heart to read their books, listen to their podcast or watch their YouTube videos, and a direct mentor is someone who has already been taught by life works with you in person to actualize your vision.

A mentor has the sole purpose of being unbiased about your potential. A mentor shares their mastery, enabling you to learn before you earn, and they approach your situation from a unique perspective. Mentors have resources, connections, and a vested interest in seeing you succeed, yet they are far enough removed to not have a legally binding responsibility to the organization—they cannot be held liable for your decisions and course of action for simply given advice. Keep in mind, I'm not speaking about a Board of Directors here, I'm referring to mentors, counsel or advisors—I'm referring to tapping into experiential information.

Mentors are one great way to learn before earning, but mentor relationships are limited because a mentor can only take you as far as they've gone. You may have more than one mentor throughout the course of your business depending on the season the business is in and how passionate you are about pursuing potential. I recall during my first year in the industry, there was a man who I heard about was working in real estate with annual sales of +$80 million dollars. I aspired to have those numbers too. I called him and asked if he would mentor me, and he responded "start with someone who's making $1M, when you reach that find someone making $5M, so on so forth. When you get past $30M, then give me a call." I was offended with his response, not realizing that he just gave me steps to follow (an attribute of a mentor). His phase philosophy is how he got to where he is at. Embrace the process and realize your mentorship relationships can help grow your business and should do just that.

The widow had a launch stage (startup) mentorship relationship with Elisha, the accountability made her focus on attaining and accomplishing her goals. The widow acknowledges this mentorship relationship in that the Bible states that the widow checked in with Elisha after she followed all of his instructions, verse seven reads "She went and told the man of God, and he said, "Go, sell the oil and pay your debts. You and your sons can live on what is left." The widow isn't mentioned after verse seven again, she had a nice startup but now needed a growth strategy mentor because the relationship with Elisha gave her a hot fast paced startup which made her a top selling oil rep in her region and the widow had a better relationship with Elisha than her husband. It's evident in that she saw the results from the instruction and application. It's said that standing too close to someone, you don't see them clearly. Keep your mentor close enough to be able to receive and not too close to take for granted.

Elisha was a very powerful man of God, and through his relationship with God (and his relationship with his mentor - Elijah) he learned that God will supply all the widows needs according to God's riches and glory. Because of this belief system, Elisha was able to convey sternly and confidently that the widow would be well if she listened to the direction of her mentor. Elisha's mentor, Elijah, had a similar experience with a widow in 1 Kings 17:8-16 ESV, "Then the word of the LORD came to him, 'Arise, go to Zarephath, which belongs to Sidon, and dwell there. Behold, I have commanded a widow there to feed you.'" So he rose and went to Zarephath. When he came to the gate of the city, a widow was there gathering sticks. He called to her and said, "Bring me a little water in a vessel that I may drink." As she was going to bring it, he called to her and said, "Bring me a morsel of bread in your hand." She said, 'As the LORD your God lives, I have nothing baked, only a handful of flour in a jar and a little oil in a jug. And now I am gathering a couple of sticks that I may go in and prepare it for myself and my son, that we may eat it and die." And Elijah said to her, "Do not fear; go and do as you have said. But first make me a little cake of it and bring it to me, and afterward make something for yourself and your son. For thus says the Lord, the God of Israel, 'The jar of flour shall not be spent, and the jug of oil shall not be empty, until the day that the Lord sends rain upon the earth.'" She went and did as Elijah said. She and he and her household ate for many days. The jar of flour was not spent, neither did the jug of oil become empty, according to the word of the Lord that he spoke through Elijah.

Isn't that interesting that the two; Elijah and Elisha, both dealt with widows and oil? Since Elisha had someone to mentor and coach him, with a similar experience, he was confident that the same God who performed a similar miracle can perform it again (indifferent to circumstance). Once that realization collided with the demand placed on Elisha's lap, he spoke boldly into the widow's future— "if you do this, you will see this!"

One of the problems millennials face is the inability to form direct mentorship relationships because we've learned to communicate in 160 characters and by isolated thought patterns throughout a period of time. There are endless possibilities within 160 characters but there are infinite opportunities beyond the box—start online (gather information, make connections, and follow influencers with information you need), continue offline - meeting people and building relationships in business (specifically established in pursuit) can tip the scale to your advantage.

In 2 Kings 4:2-7 NIV, the single mother sought advice which could provide a solution for an ongoing issue - she had no direction, was extremely motivated to do something, but didn't know where to start. Have you ever been there? Motivated to see change in your business but not sure how to start, where to start or who can help? To be perfectly honest, writing this book has been, at times; scary, uncertain, and painful - not the writing part as much as the finishing part. Where do I go for editing? What's the best approach, print, digital or both?

Who should publish, who's the best publisher for this type of book? Or, do I self-publish? Also, should I translate to Spanish on initial release or wait a few months? There were so many questions and I had to seek direction from people who been where I'd like to go; be it as an entrepreneur or as an author.

Throughout my process, I identified with these women. I felt confused, frustrated, scared, insecure and limited - I didn't know enough to impact and because I couldn't impact, I couldn't influence. The widow's conversation with the man of God challenged her thinking and renewed her mind. Information does that, it challenges what you think but most importantly are the mentors that make you realize the challenge is possible. Remember, a mentor's function is to inform you and learning does not have an expiration date and you're held accountable for what you know. You cannot place yourself at a disadvantage in lieu of your potential because you are ashamed, afraid or insecure to ask a question or ask for assistance. The widow had the right idea, "I need help" and what she got in return was worth more than what she believed she would have received. "Wisdom is obtained by two methods; buying or borrowing it." - Benjamin Franklin; note that most people love to tell their story, some may charge but there are some who won't - it's all about your approach, additionally we purchase lessons direct from life through the acts of our flesh because the wages of sin are death - some people prefer to learn the hard way. I hope you will find solace in the borrowing approach.

In chaos and fear, her life was about to take on new responsibility, but she didn't know that. Imagine this, she's coming for help in one area because she has no money and her "mentor" fires back- "well, actually, I advise you to start a business, you have an anointing that can really unlock doors for you if you put it to work and follow the steps I'm about to give you!" How would you respond? Here I am telling you, you have an anointing, if you cultivate it and perfect it, you'll press oil. Take your oil in front of a mentor, you'll have accountability and direction.

Now, depending on how serious you take this counsel we can classify you as a chaser or a runner. Will you abandon the path towards your success because it seems daunting or because you expected a hand-out and received a business model?

The widow showed us that a good mentor will direct in the path that will require more of you while a handout will never develop your ability but will always leave you in debt!

The Competitive Advantage

Information distinguishes and grants authority, the Bible reads in Hosea 4:6 NIV that "My people are destroyed from lack of knowledge. Because you have rejected knowledge I also reject you as my priests; because you have ignored the law of your God, I also will ignore your children." Here's the thing about knowledge and ignorance, it is a generational advantage or disadvantage. The information gained by self-learning or mentorship expedites your mastery, and if applied, will be with you until you're able to pass it along—with some additional information that you gathered along your own journey. So, when your son or daughter, niece or nephew says, "I want to own my own business," you'll be able to give tips to help them become specialist. Specialist are paid more, because a consumer pays for a problem to be solved-those who solve faster get referrals and can ask for more. The real breakthrough occurs when the information received challenges the information currently on file.

Growth is so uncomfortable, it causes a person to check in with people from the past who aren't privy to the new information. We'll ask a parent, who having our best interest at heart, gives us direction based on their understanding of who we were (the child they raised, in the community we grew up in) not based on the path we've decided to pursue, so their advice may be helpful and protective but may also not be the solution. Sometimes we look to our friends to help guide our ideas, people whose lives practically mirror where we are but no longer want to be and we ask them to help us make a decision that will direct our next course of action. These people will give us their opinion without having any experience that can support their answer. I remember my wife asked me to design the shirts and hats for P'Lacio's - to wear when we use to transform our home to a restaurant on Saturdays, I wanted the hats to look cool and shirts to be something that people would wear when not working as a way of helping us spread the message. So, I take this hat to a friend after we get them designed and embroidered, he looks as the hat and says, "I like it, they're nice, but maybe switch the name because no one will wear someone else's name on their body." I was bothered by our interaction, at one point I found myself thinking, I thought this was like a brother? A few weeks later I mention to my wife how discouraged I got and I started to think about that night again and remembered my friend having on a pair of Jordan shoes and some other name brand clothing. I recall thinking, how dare I let this man distort what I know God has shown me? Since that time, we haven't spoken much about any project I work on, there aren't any feelings of resentment and frustrations—instead I took the experience and became very protective of who I allow to have input or how I receive opinions regarding the information I have. There are criteria I use to judge if someone's input is credible and noteworthy, if the criteria isn't met then I don't ask for their idea, opinion, feedback or direction. When the wrong source provides insight at a critical moment the outcome disrupts decision making opportunities which can be pivotal turning points for your business—choose who you listen to wisely.

In Proverbs 15:22 NIV, King Solomon teaches us that "Plans fail for lack of counsel, but with many advisers they succeed." It's ironic that the book of Proverbs is King Solomon (literally) teaching his son how to conduct himself as royalty, teaching that by having a team to counsel you through running your kingdom the kingdom will not depart from him (in today's world we call these people our board of advisors).

King Solomon's son's name is Rehoboam, let's briefly review his story to illustrate why wise counsel is very important: in 1 Kings 12:4-11 MSG Rehoboam becomes King and ushers a new era in Israel. The people come to him to voice their concerns "Your father made life hard for us-worked our fingers to the bone. Give us a break, lighten up on us and we'll willingly serve you." Rehoboam responds by saying "give me three days to think this over, then come back." Within those three days he asked the elders (wise counsel) and their response is "show empathy, respond with compassion, and they'll commit to your leadership, honoring their word to serve you." Rehoboam rejects their response and seeks counsel from friends, the Bible says, "the young turks who he'd grown up with." These friends advised him to be tougher and to respond that his "little finger is thicker than his father's waist... my father thrashed you with whips, I'll beat you bloody with chains!" Needless to say, that day he lost 2/3 of the Kingdom God gave to his grandfather David and his father Solomon and retained Judah only. Wrong words at the right moment from friends, two of my criteria is that our relationship has to be new and my advisor must have 10 years of experience (minimal) in which there has been continual growth and adjustments (personal and professional) within the last seven years (I focus on the last seven years because I believe it takes three years for a business to really get going).

Your Kingdom may be your business or your idea for a business, the difference between a launch and never launching may very well be the people you're listening to. Experience also lends to EQ.

Own Your Development

I want to share what King Solomon said in the Book of Proverbs regarding securing your development before moving forward with a decision:

Proverbs 1:5 NIV - Let the wise listen and add to their learning, and let the discerning get guidance

Proverbs 11:14 NIV - For lack of guidance a nation falls, but victory is won through many advisers

Proverbs 15:22 NIV - Plans fail for lack of counsel, but with many advisers they succeed

Proverbs 20:18 NIV - Plans are established by seeking advice; so if you wage war, obtain guidance.

Proverbs 24:6 NIRV - If you go to war, you need guidance. If you want to win, you need many good advisers.

The common theme that Solomon is sharing is simple: your oil, its process, your finances, marriage, and life are much stronger when you have a someone willingly educating and sharing insight, can hold you accountable, and develop your IQ and EQ-which develops your bottom-line. Always, learn before you earn.

Lesson 2: Without counsel plans fail, but with many advisers they succeed. Proverbs 15:22

2a: It's not a sign of weakness to get advice. In doing so, make sure your advice is from someone with experience in what you're building!

CHAPTER 3

Hubbard Lake

Hubbard Lake is a favorite vacation spot for Michiganders, fishing is what you do there. From Ypsilanti, it's roughly a four-hour drive but that's not the point, you go to Hubbard Lake to fish and relax - I'm not much of a fisherman but I understand the parallels (whether sales and marketing or networking) - if you want bass you throw a line where bass are. In 2 Kings 4:3 NIV - Elisha said, "Go around and ask all your neighbors for empty jars. Don't ask for just a few." She's about to go fishing!

Once you realize how valuable time is, you realize how much of it is maximized once you learn to allocate. One can quickly confuse progress with movement and circle the same mountain day in and day out for years until it finally dawns that the time it took you building your site or learning tax laws, could have been invested in cultivating your gift. You haven't progressed, you just know a lot.

At this moment, I didn't know exactly what to do and I applied my mentor's advice of cooking out of our kitchen (every Saturday our kitchen and dining room became a restaurant) but my wife and I were ready for the big leagues - we just didn't have the resources or the know-how. In Harvey Mackay's book *Dig Your Well Before You're Thirsty*, you learn why networking and building relationships can take you where you need to be or help you when you need it most. In the book, there's a top-ten list of the most important things a network can do;

1. A network replaces the weakness of an individual with the strength of the group
2. Gives you accountability; making you aware of how things look or sound (like a mirror)
3. Shows you who your friends and enemies are
4. Helps you connect with a bigger network
5. A big network can enrich your life anywhere in the world
6. Gives information and insight through information and knowledge
7. Can help you help others
8. Protects you against job insecurity
9. Makes you look good
10. Expands your financial reach

Wasn't that the truth! First let me clarify, these relationships are not to be mistaken with mentorship relationships and not to be mistaken with employees - these are relationships that help you stay a master because they fill the gaps - CPA, IP attorney, grant writer, website designer, etc... As an entrepreneur, these relationships are resourceful, but you must *find* them. For me, preparing myself for fishing required attending a few BNI meetings, and becoming more social at the gym, work, and church - to be frank, you cannot do it all. You'll never move forward to the grand opening.

You must get to the point where the conversation is different about your business, I hated hearing "man that's a great idea," I wanted to hear "can you quote a catering opportunity for a wedding with 300 guests?" My decision was simple, either we stay stuck or I start to pack the hook, lines, net, and spear. Once that decision was made the importance of each player became priority. Our CPA played a more intricate role than simply doing our taxes, eventually becoming a real friend to our family who understood the vision and connected the dots. Also, we started to establish relationships with a grant program who introduced us to architects and commercial Realtors in Detroit.

These relationships are great to have, and you want to stay on the good side, but you will not always need their services. For example, the consulting agency gave me a new template for the business plan and helped me work on my elevator pitch - they were very instrumental in getting us funded through Motor City Match, our CPA literally saved us from the biggest headaches to date and consulted the company in areas of taxes, especially with the new tax laws.

Networking and Your Entrepreneurial Personality Type

You have to be patient to go fishing, fish don't always bite. When they do bite, then ask yourself what type of fisherman are you? Fishing to feed yourself or fishing to sell (maximizing the relationship). Regarding your business, networking can help you strengthen your weaknesses and build bridges and tunnels. The more you allocate, the more time you must specialize - and when you're special, you're paid different. Therefore, when you network, match yourself correctly. For example, if you classify yourself as a chaser architect, you may want to work with a chaser who specializes in website design, to ensure your dollar is well spent. If you consider yourself a runner auto repair guru, pair with a chaser for balance. A runner wants his/her concept to take off on day one, they work hard but they also abandon quick - they're ambitious but committed through a series of quick wins. While a chaser is like a farmer, s/he sows in a flood and in a drought, they understand that if they keep planting, they will reap a harvest.

There are positives and negatives for both personalities; one positive for a runner is their passion and belief - my experience as a runner is that I've abandoned ideas but never abandoned the goal. Let me explain, perhaps the goal is employing at least 50 people with competitive, livable wages, empowering those 50 to pursue their entrepreneurial passions while building up a "new 50" and the idea was to invest time, money and energy in a multi-level marketing company to meet the goal. The runner will bounce from idea to idea until they find the correct platform that fits their need and personality and they experience its payout. A con for a runner will be that they become known as a jack of all trades, people stop wanting to talk to them because they went from "friend" to client and are always being sold to.

A positive for a chaser will be their ability to pour all their energy into one thing until it succeeds, while negatives would include their inability to delegate (initially). See, nobody's perfect but it is important to classify yourself, so you can see where you lack and reach out for help.

Your oil is strengthened by your team, I can't emphasize this enough. The relationships you build perfect your anointing, give you exposure and introduce you to new partners with bigger, deeper resources. Don't just hire an accountant to do your taxes, hire one that has experience in your field and one that has resources and connections that can help connect you.

Our accountant has over 30 years of experience and our lawyer over 40, that's 70 years of experience making sure we're covered. Sure, they may have other clients or are invested in other areas besides their main profession but at the core they've stuck to one thing for an extended period of time. They've had bad years and great years but kept planting and established a name for themselves. Credibility can't be purchased, it must be established - so if you're a runner look for time. If you're a chaser, look for other chasers as well. In other areas such as marketing and technology I encourage you to work with companies that have helped more than one client succeed-because the landscapes of marketing and technology evolves often, it would benefit you to partner with a hybrid chaser, one who is a student of their industry but also knows about more than just one aspect of their industry.

Extra Virgin Oil

Extra virgin olive oil is the best olive oil. The olives are crushed at a mill and the oil is extracted via machines versus heat and chemicals. When I learned that, I thought to myself - it takes time to produce the best. Same goes for working with the right people, establishing partnerships isn't an easy concept and it isn't something you should "just do." The right person performing the wrong function, in your business, is as good as having hired no one at all while the wrong person doing exactly what is needed - may have an alternate motive. Partnering, is also difficult because entrepreneurs see an opportunity and attempt the resolution ourselves. It's our inevitable gift and our unforgiving shortcoming - chasers excel in creating functional partnerships because they take the time to cultivate the relationship and carve the fit to be a perfect match, they can inspect what they expect, then coach up instead of coaching out! Chasers are great at partnering with the need versus the want, always partnering with people smarter and leveraging relationships- with integrity, leveraging the relationships.

Cultivate the Relationship

Your business can leverage greatly from relationships, think long term—these are not overnight manifestations. Find people smarter than you in your areas of weakness, ask them for help, be open to the idea that this relationship may cost you (financially), and confront your weakness. You are as strong as the weakest link in your chain, but what do you do when you are the weakest link? God has blessed us with an amazing idea to introduce Panamanian and Honduran street food, but I excel in marketing and management; what happens if I'm forced to function outside of my area of expertise having to do the taxes? All bad, I should be aware and alert of tax laws and implications but not the person leading that area.

Allow for clarification, weakness doesn't take away from what you do bring to the table, but you do not have the time and the resources to be focused on anything other than perfecting the recipes. All other areas are your weaknesses; acknowledge and address them - know what's going on, have input in the process but have confidence in your ability to hire the correct person.

Cultivating the relationship means to acquire, develop, then prepare for use. In other words, you must network, you must be transparent and authentic then you must ask for assistance. Proverbs 28:19 MSG says, "work your garden-you'll end up with plenty of food; play and party-you'll end up with an empty plate." The Millennial Kingdom translation is *those who fish and work their network will have plenty of resources, while those who run after fantasies and abandons structure will be impoverished.* There are no shortcuts.

Inspect What You Expect

You know what you want to see, what you hope to have your team accomplish and what you expect from each player on your team, but how are you managing those needs? Your management of these relationships is based solely on the functionality of the performance of the task, not of the person themselves. Then you must adjust to find the perfect fit. People are people, we aren't perfect, and we aren't mistake-proof you cannot micromanage a person because it will discourage them from performing the task. Genesis chapter 1 teaches us that we were to dominate Earth not people, this goes back to your oil and your gift. You know what it is now make sure you're surrounded with the right relationships that will bring it forth.

Here's an example of inspecting what you expect, we started to create and learn how to have our plantain chips placed in stores. So, as I reach out to a few buyers and suppliers, it was our job to make sure we were able to get the right people in place to one, keep it organic and to teach us along the way. It was a new venture and different terrain. It is my responsibility to inspect if using Company X as a supplier will be best suited for our vision. In addition, our Food Safety Plan requires us to know every aspect of the process, such as where the plantains are coming from and the funnel goes through before we buy them. Are there chemicals being used or not? It is not my responsibility to argue, curse and criticize when we simply have to move and match, "I understand you don't believe in xyz, we don't feel our visions are best suited for each other now but maybe in the near future. Unfortunately, we have to part ways - thank you for the opportunity." My job is to manage; inspect what I expect from my anointing which God gave me to perfect to have dominion.

Coach Up, Not Coach Out

My mentor would to tell me, "don't throw the baby out with the bathwater" - honestly had no idea what he was talking about the first time I heard it. I laughed and asked "*what*?!?" He never explained, but I learned - we hired a gentleman to work at a company my mentor owned, and I managed. After discussing bringing this person on board with another member of our leadership team (who was a mutual friend of the applicant) the recommendation made this person appear perfect but after a while we realized that this person produced no results, so I would micromanage the person instead of the function we needed. Long story short, it got to where I couldn't ask for anything from this person without an argument ensuing. It got to where the person would only do what my mentor would ask, problem with that is my mentor asked me to lead the company - it discredited me in the eyes of my mentor.

To coach up and not coach out means to remind yourself, we're here to dominate Earth using our gifting and it is our responsibility to effectively fill roles that will aide in accomplishing the goal. Your job is to coach the role or bridge the gap-hold the need accountable, not micromanage the individual. Remember, that role will outlast that person if you build your vision correctly. So, which role needs to perform better? Who is currently in this role? Can we find a new role for this person or can we explain / make the process different, so this person can fulfil what is required at that role using the talents, resources and abilities they have access to versus making them perform as someone they are not?

There are tons of examples of this in our everyday life, sometimes we tend to coach out; saying a person simply doesn't fit and instead of finding a place in the vision they will fit, perfectly, we get rid of them entirely. Not every instance requires complete separation, perhaps the PR agency you hired isn't great with PPC marketing, but they'll get you press and TV spots, or your business lawyer can also be your accountant, but you determine that what your company needs from this person is to focus solely on corporate law. Be ok with coaching up, first.

Ever Been Married?

I've been married twice... in business. The first time I had no idea what the divorce would be like—it hurt, this was a person I trusted, split money with, went to their kids' birthday parties and shared visions, ideas, food with. We were so busy building our business that we would work late while our wives would call us upset because we should be at home. For meetings, we would take our kids out with us-one will sit in the car with the kids, the other would knock out the meeting. I never imagined that we wouldn't be working together—we divorced, and the business crumbled because we both started as runners, as God started to renew my mind and the Holy Spirit started to show me that I had to stick it out, my partner remained a runner and was already gone. The business was in real estate and here we are hungry and excited, but we didn't have enough time in - there were just some things we didn't know. Then there's my second marriage, but I learned from the first one - so we signed a prenuptial agreement. It is my business and you work for me, but I'll pay you very well, almost as a partner until you can prove yourself to be a partner. The lesson here was that I wasn't the owner, just the manager.

Modern business culture has taught us to get rid of a person quick but what if the person was perfectly fine and your idea was underdeveloped? Evaluate everything before calling it quits, chasers get this concept well. They are in for the long haul, they understand that the role is more important than the person in it and aren't married to the person but are to the role. Since they aren't married to the person but are to the role, they understand that whoever fits the role needs to be able to fit the current need of that role and are willing to separate from the person or adjust the role to fit the person.

Yes, I said "current need of the role," why? Well as you grow your needs should change - same is true in life as it is in your business. As you grow, you will change - I consulted for a restaurant owner and asked the owner what is the restaurant's goal for next quarter, the owner quickly responded "hiring more people," mentioning that upon opening the location there was too many people working and not enough clientele but now the problem has reversed, there are hardly enough staff and the customer service has performed poorly. My suggestion to the owner was to not throw the baby out with the bath water. There's an obvious need and immediate urgency but remember, wrong people on the right function could be like hiring no one at all and just throwing good money after bad. I encouraged filling the most important roles first by coaching up within while interviewing outside applicants-it will give time to find the right fit while seeing who on the team currently is mature enough to handle a leadership role.

Power in Numbers

Henry Ford (world renowned entrepreneur and founder of Ford motor company) is quoted as saying "Coming together is a beginning; keeping together is progress; working together is success." The illustration of this single mother is more common today than ever; I was raised in a single mother led household, secondly there are 10 million single mother-led families in the United States, three-times that of the 1960s. Therefore, when it comes to growing your idea into a [profitable] business (whether the idea was birthed from necessity or creativity) - if these women could do it and if my mother could do it, so could you. The keys (DJ Khaled voice) are to follow instruction and assemble a team to carry out this mission.

Let's look at another example of partnership and relationship where desperation and faith caused change and ushered in results Mark 2:3-4 ESV

"And they came, bringing to him a paralytic carried by four men. And when they could not get near him because of the crowd, they (the four men) removed the roof above him, and when they had made an opening, they let down the bed on which the paralytic lay."

All great ideas, will eventually, need a team to reach its potential, never get this misunderstood. The illustration above shows that a good team will be there for each other and prioritize concepts until the group reaches its expected end.

In Habakkuk chapter 2 verse 2 NIV, the author writes "Then the LORD replied: "Write down the revelation and make it plain on tablets so that a herald may run with it." Once you establish your team, one of the primary functions will be to present a clear and concise vision of the objections for the business and their roles. This will enable the team to have great synergy and the individuals to contribute effectively in their area of strength.

God Established Relationships

It's not good for man to be alone while he's taking dominion, you can accomplish much more in teams (and partnerships) than you can individually, this is God established! Not all partnerships have a cost associated but some will, yet the goal should be consistent—the good of the business.

In Genesis 1:26-30 NIV and Genesis 2:15 NIV, God made man in His image and likeness, gave man an identity, dominion and a function. In Genesis 2:18-24 NIV, God gives man help. This concept of "no man is an island" was established by God during creation, we make entrepreneurship more difficult than it needs to be by a spirit called pride that says, "I can do this by myself."

Lesson 3: It's not good to be alone, on the other side of your oil there is a group of people you'll need to prepare you for distribution

3a: Together Everyone Achieves More

CHAPTER 4

Opportunity Cost

*"Prioritizing activities to accomplish goals is
a good way to avoid the distraction
of performing duties which yield no return
on your investment of time.
Focus on potential producing activities, only."*

- Odell Palacio

Resources are scarce, relative to needs. So, the use of resources in one way prevents their use in others. Money, ideas, and time are the Holy Trinity of resources for entrepreneurs, of these, time is the most valuable resource you have access to! Everything is time based and time sensitive, but you cannot manage time you can only manage what you do with time, simply because we are all awarded the same amount of it. Therefore; we can say time is a currency and how we spend time determines our outcome. All our efforts have a direct correlation in exchange for, thus; the activities you pursue, given an allotted amount of time, has an equivalent response. Let me elaborate a bit, let's assume you're working a regular job while developing your business idea, you also have other responsibilities throughout the day, in addition to sleeping, cooking, eating, and cleaning - in this scenario, let's assume you have one hour to develop your business (or press your oil), daily. What you do with that hour has its results in direct proportion, if you place cold calls during that time, write your business plan, work on digital marketing, read a book, create a logo, buy from Alibaba to sell on Amazon or eBay, go out to eat with friends, or watch TV, you get what you put in. Thus, the idea of opportunity cost is vastly important when considering activity management in view of time resource.

The concept of time is interesting for entrepreneurs, I have a colleague that reads (and recommends) every entrepreneur and self-help book on the market while most of his time is invested at his 9 - 5. Although he recommends often, he applies hardly. I wonder if he realizes that if he maximizes the free time he has after his shift ends and he settles in for the day, he could yield great results for his business. He's a musician with a studio in his basement but no music for the public. What we focus on expands, I encourage you to evaluate where you're at and ask yourself if your time could be used more wisely.

We'll discuss two concepts in this chapter; one is called opportunity cost, and the other is called paradigms, I want there to be an understanding of these two concepts, so progress and movement could stop being confused. One is to know that there's always an alternative, and resource management, especially regarding time, is really about activity (or what you do) versus time itself - we're all given 24 hours. The other is the "why," as millennial entrepreneurs, we often choose the alternatives.

An opportunity cost is a benefit, profit, or value of something that must be given up acquiring or achieve something else. Since every resource (land, money, time, etc.) can be put to alternative uses, every action, choice, or decision has an associated opportunity cost. Opportunity cost is an economic term, another definition is the loss of potential gain from other alternatives when one alternative is chosen. Remember, this chapter isn't about time management it's about activity management; as a theory that is what opportunity cost is. How you manage your resources, what activities you partake in. Jesus explained it in the Parable of the Talents where the resource was money and time, but activity determined the results; let us review Matthew 25:14-29 NIRV:

"Again, here is what the kingdom of heaven will be like. A man was going on a journey. He sent for his servants and put them in charge of his property. He gave $10,000 to one. He gave $4,000 to another. And he gave $2,000 to the third. The man gave each servant the amount of money he knew the servant could take care of. Then he went on his journey. "The servant who had received the $10,000 went at once and put his money to work. He earned $10,000 more. The one with the $4,000 earned $4,000 more. But the man who had received $2,000 went and dug a hole in the ground. He hid his master's money in it. "After a long time, the master of those servants returned. He wanted to collect all the money they had earned. The man who had received $10,000 brought the other $10,000. 'Master,' he said, 'you trusted me with $10,000. See, I have earned $10,000 more.' "His master replied, 'You have done well, good and faithful servant! You have been faithful with a few things. I will put you in charge of many things. Come and share your master's happiness!' "The man with $4,000 also came. 'Master,' he said, 'you trusted me with $4,000. See, I have earned $4,000 more.' "His master replied, 'You have done well, good and faithful servant! You have been faithful with a few things. I will put you in charge of many things. Come and share your master's happiness!' "Then the man who had received $2,000 came. 'Master,' he said, 'I knew that you are a hard man. You harvest where you have not planted. You gather crops where you have not scattered seed. So, I was afraid. I went out and hid your $2,000 in the ground. See, here is what belongs to you.' "His master replied, 'You evil, lazy servant! So you knew that I harvest where I have not planted? You knew that I gather crops where I have not scattered seed? Well then, you should have put my money in the bank. When I returned, I would have received it back with interest.' "Then his master commanded the other servants, 'Take the $2,000 from him. Give it to the one who has $20,000. Everyone who has will be given more. He will have more than enough. And what about anyone who doesn't have? Even what he has will be taken away from him.

Opportunity cost is synonymous with value and maturity - according to the scripture above, "the man gave each servant the amount of money he knew the servant could take care of." Thus, according to their proportion, one values the resource and the has the maturity to multiply their flow. Here's what happens when you mismanage what you should value, you lose it. Ever had more month than money? Not enough time in a day? Lost a client?

Elisha speaking in 2 Kings 4:4-5 NIV, 4 Then go inside and *shut the door behind you and your sons.* Pour oil into all the jars, and as each is filled, put it to one side.

5 She left him and *shut the door behind her and her sons.*

There are always options, but value and maturity generate focus. Your story may not be as extreme as possibly losing your sons to debt, but you may be close to foreclosing on your home or having the car repossessed, what's your fight or flight response? Are you going to sit and eat a bunch of ice cream while crying or are you going to pour oil in each jar?

Elaboration of the "door"

What did Elisha mean to say with "Shut the door" and did you notice the display of obedience? As a matter of fact, this incident is grouped with other instructions and part of information that is life changing and an influential factor in her startup's success, while the other is an act of completion, worthy of success. 1 Samuel 15:22 NLT states obedience is better than sacrifice, and submission is better than offering.

I believe the phrase "shut the door" means to eliminate all [possible] distraction(s). This is an education on the value of the time and the Man of God is driving a point that we miss as millennials. Our generation is the greatest generation the world has ever seen (regarding the access to information). We're also a distracted generation, the tools which were meant to connect us has been used by some to drive us apart. What you value you esteem and try not to waste. It's hard to get children to honor a gift or a toy. They want the toy so much but once they get it - they may play with it a few times, break it then abandon it, why? They didn't esteem and value it, they were not invested in the purchasing aspect of it - money (an asset), time (an asset), ideas (an asset); but time is the most important!

In the case of the single mother, once time is valued, and there's an acknowledgement of the main objective, which is to avoid the creditor from taking her sons - then shutting the door is an obvious step to not avoid while the luxury of mis-budgeting time is not. What we miss, often, is this habitual behavior we must choose leisure versus the awakening which occurs when there is focus and emotion on one task, because subconsciously millennials are taught to be distracted, those who value time and have laser sharp focus on their goal - take a chaser's approach and usually perform until the desired outcome is produced.

A poor single mother turned entrepreneur forced to acknowledge her oil (anointing) and encouraged to take the chaser approach to starting her first business, she became an entrepreneur through tragedy and got more than she bargained for while seeking a handout! Notwithstanding, what was on the other side of that door? Why was there such an emphasis from the man of God's instruction, "shut the door behind you and your sons?" In this case, a lot of time has already been invested entertaining fear and doubt - we know that fear paralyzes, and doubt procrastinates. The opportunity cost of entertaining those two emotions any further would result in slavery as debt repaid. Had she skipped a step outlined by her mentor, she would have paralyzed the potential of her launch and procrastinated the manifestation of her outcome.

A door symbolizes an entrance and an exit -the man of God was saying, at this very moment you need nobody or nothing coming in and out of your life, mind, spirit, and atmosphere you need to visualize the potential of your anointing and by shutting the door you can maximize activity time. She's a single mother widow who, for the entirety of her marriage, did not work because her husband managed the household finances. Now she's forced to tap into her oil, quickly. During the time of this scripture, historically, there was an occupation entitled professional mourners (or paid mourners) in the Mediterranean region, these people (usually women), would get paid to cry - they would be at the funeral, at the house, on the streets, crying for pay - no real attachment (Jeremiah 9:17-18 NIRV). Add that to the stress of the creditor, the ridicule of her neighbors and family (before and after she asked for bottles), while fighting her own emotions and confusion. In between success and failure is decision, she could entertain or overcome by one decision; shut the door, maximize your activity.

Occupying the Dreams of Others

I couldn't settle for what I was told I was worth or when I should go on lunch, break or talk. That is not God's will for me. I'm not opposed, nor do I encourage the reader to not work for anyone, instead, find an opportunity that allows the flexibility to still pursue your goals or where you can pour all your oil into your role and get paid to do so. A job that will let you get commission (uncapped) or where you wake up passionate daily.

Me University

I confused long days with productivity, I was not entirely productive and [learning from my mistakes] I realized I could honestly get to bed much sooner. I like to think long term, I like to look at the future and see its possibility and plan; one of my plans is to die empty, a theme Dr. Myles Munroe teaches throughout his works. The saying means to pour out your purpose, to leave an impact and an inheritance, not to look back wishing you could have done something and be envious of those who have. That's exactly where I am in life right now; telling myself "I must die empty." Perhaps it's a bad thought, I can see the dichotomy in it because you're almost calling something to be before its destined time. Nevertheless, I come at it from an urgency point of view, I've wasted time before, and I didn't optimize opportunities because of my comfort with time. I've been distracted, I've mismanaged, and I didn't value or was mature.

I didn't recognize that how I budgeted time reflects my values and oftentimes, I have exchanged prime moments in my day to watch other people make history (so I could be a part of the water cooler conversation in the morning).

By no means am I saying it's wrong to know about current events, but in my story I had to stop caring about everything else besides my family and my purpose, I found myself constantly playing catch up - I got to a point where I got tired of having good ideas and being around people with good ideas. I wanted to be around people with good execution, people I could learn from. My first course of action was to write down my distractions,

There are many day to day activities that can be qualified as distractions but shutting the door wasn't easy. Some things I had to fight were distractions such as; validation, TV, food, social media, church, and job / career. I'll talk a little bit about a few of these but what I encourage you to do now is identify your distraction by name, write down how it distracts you, how you were introduced to it and what you could be doing instead of it. It may seem hard, but it isn't, you'll learn a lot about yourself.

Types of distractions to be aware of

Phones / Social Media

The first cell phone was created April 3, 1973, a decade later, September 21, 1983, Motorola sold the 8000X, which cost consumers $3,995. I was surprised by this information, the world moves so fast now one week feels like eternity and just to think that these technological advances are still new, not even that old.

Nevertheless, the first smartphone (IBM Simon) was sold August 16, 1994. In 1997, Six Degrees, became the world's first recognizable social media site. In 1999 blogging became popular and by the 2000s social media began to explode in popularity. Myspace and LinkedIn gained prominence in the early 2000s, our first Instagram were sites like Photobucket and Flickr, then YouTube came out in 2005, creating an entirely new way for people to communicate and share with each other across great distances.

By 2006, Facebook and Twitter both became available to users throughout the world. These sites remain some of the most popular social networks. Other sites like Tumblr, Spotify, Foursquare and Pinterest began popping up to fill specific social networking niches. For nearly five decades, some of us have allowed for ourselves to disconnect from our goals to 'Like' and 'share' in the advancements of others.

I made this comment to a friend, "cell phones have become my best and worst ally!" I've found myself at times - in between projects, "taking a break" and using my phone to do so. What I would hope to be a few moments would turn into a lack of production for several minutes, maybe even hours. I believe what you mismanage will be taken away from you.

Job / Career

The function of a job (just over broke) is to help you develop skills related to your oil, learn to work with others, and earn money to invest in your oil. For many people, a job doesn't bring fulfillment - mostly we're working more than one job (or overtime at the job) to afford a lifestyle. A job has an expiration date (you either quit, retire, get fired, or laid off) but your ideas have no expiration date or unemployment line. The problem is, we come home from working and we're "tired," inspired only to eat, watch TV and sleep and our belief is we're doing the right thing, recharging the battery (just to do it all again the next day).

I really believe we were all placed on this earth to add value and dominate in our area of gifting and that God has placed in each one of us a unique vision when we close our eyes. This vision (or idea) is what you acknowledge in your heart to be who you are destined to become; it may be a school teacher with a progressive method for reaching at-risk students or a chef with a new restaurant concept, an engineer, musician, architect, pastor, political figure or a biochemist with the cure to AIDS - one thing or certain, you know who LeBron James is.

In regard to the tiredness you feel when you get home from work, that feeling isn't an overwhelming exhaust from the rigors of your work day, it's a lack of inspiration because you're working a j.o.b., that isn't what you see when you close your eyes. This frustration leads to criticism of those making the most of their time, we tweet about them, post about them or "like" comments about them while harboring disgust and angst about the very existence we've created for ourselves. For the record, I'm not opposed to working a 9 - 5, but encourage you to maximize your 5 - 9. The bible puts it this way in Ecclesiastes 11:6 NIRV: "In the morning plant your seeds. In the evening keep your hands busy. You don't know what will succeed. It may be one or the other. Or both might do equally well." What that means is go to work in the morning, pay your rent! In the evening, work on your business.

Don't leave your day job till your evening efforts take off or have a mean side hustle and keep working both.

Validation

The allure and addiction of validation causes a person to behave, repeatedly, in a manner seeking of approval from man rather than developing their character in Christ. Jeremiah 17:5 NIV summarizes the consequences of validation as such: "This is what the Lord says: 'Cursed is the one who trusts in man, who draws strength from mere flesh and whose heart turns away from the Lord.'"

Culturally, it is socially acceptable for the opinions of others to determine one's worth. The problem with this is that the audience doesn't applaud the rehearsal just the live show - and now you're busy comparing your rehearsal to an Oscar award winning performance (unbeknownst to you, how many hours of rehearsal went into that performance). Do not rush for applauds instead, show up and improve throughout your process - no one's opinion can expedite your process.

Your oil is enough validation - if you press and perfect it, your addiction to attention will hurt you more than promote you - Matthew 23:12 NIV says "For those who exalt themselves will be humbled, and those who humble themselves will be exalted." Your work and your character will always speak louder than your mouth.

Church

I know my church friends are going to hate this one but I'm discussing areas I had to learn to prioritize so I can maximize my activity management, getting the most out of my time! With that being said, church is awesome, find a good Bible based church that ministers the Kingdom of God and help advance the vision of the church to reach as many people as possible for Christ. Church is also a great place to build partnerships and relationships, but can church be overwhelming? It shouldn't be! It has been said that 80% of the work a church does is done by only 20% of its members. Well, what does that suggest? It means some people are doing more than one thing while others are sitting there making sure the seats don't move. Ask for help! Don't allow the spirit of apathy to creep in because that becomes an entirely different issue. Asking for help does not demonstrate weakness, it's strength.

I come to learn something about the oil God has given me, it's to expand the Kingdom. Your oil, is for you to have dominion in an area of your gifting, your oil can be productive to the church you attend. It is ideal for you to use your oil in the faithfulness of another, committed to the leader you're under, only time I believe it's okay to say "no" is if you're going to murmur. Don't allow for your oil to cause you to sin. Instead, do all things as if you're doing it for God. If you feel a complaint coming on or a murmur coming on, pull back and readjust.

What you focus on expands

Someone once told me, what I focus on magnifies, meaning it grows exponentially; thus, taking away from something else. There's a law called the law of the harvest which states "you reap what you sow." the Bible is very precise on this matter; "The point is this: whoever sows sparingly will also reap sparingly, and whoever sows bountifully will also reap bountifully." 2 Corinthians 9:6 ESV

The single mother and her two sons sowed generously, their currency was activity. What they gave up in exchange was interruption and distraction. There was a goal which challenged their perspective, the law is true, you reap what you sow. if the family ignored the Man of God's counsel, the story would have read differently. Had they ignored they would have sowed distraction and reaped poverty. Your business is dependent on your focus and self-discipline. There's no luck to this, use your time wisely so when you do pray for increase or wisdom and business tactics God will honor your prayer and see that you've been committed to the oil he gave you.

Remember this, the single mother and her children had a choice; we all have choices. You must decide what is more important to you, I told my son life will ultimately come down to choices and companionship, is about decision making.

Now you know your oil, you've spoken to your mentor, you've assembled a team, but have you made the decision to get active? I tell you a truth, the few things I've accomplished thus far were based on a decision. Here's the thing about the Law of Harvest, the result is always in direct proportion to the energy invested; if you eat poorly and sit on the couch all day you'll gain weight. If you spend more than you bring in you'll be broke, if you invest your time in revenue producing activities, you'll make revenue and lastly, if you entertain distractions you won't finish a task. The law establishes what expands or diminishes based on where focus lies. Naturally, those who focus on giving are always able to give.

Finishing your project(s) by setting goals: Manage your oil by objectives and clearly defined goals, this portion of business development is so important. When writing this book, I discovered a topic or area of interest that I felt could be elaborated on from a different perspective, wrote down the titles (and subtitles) I wanted to discuss, made a mind map for each topic to allow the thoughts to flow smoothly and lastly gave myself a deadline. Same as with your business, what is your business? What are your areas you want to tackle? What will it take tackle each area? What is your deadline? Once you do this, turn off the TV, smartphone, ignore calls from friends and get focused.

Broken Things

Just because something is broken, doesn't mean it can't be fixed. May just need some TLC. Interestingly enough; the biggest gulf between your business launching and your to-do list is called attitude. How you view your to-do list determines how you value your time. Be a chaser, think long term and think progressive. By avoiding the to-do list only increases its length, daily. If you have to call someone to price quote signage for your business plan, then guess what? It must get done. Eliminate distractions, don't give them an opportunity; it's just a matter of adjustment.

The Bible declares that all creation is waiting eagerly for that future day when God will reveal who his children really are Romans 8:19 NLT. There is someone out there waiting on your destiny and once you start to get busy, your work will testify on the greatness of the God you serve. Yet, how will you ever get to your potential if you have not identified that you have a pot of oil you can use hidden behind a wall of distractions or set aside while you scroll Instagram? It is never too late to get started, as long as you have breath in your lungs, you have destiny.

Paradigms. A paradigm is defined as a model; or pattern of something - A mental program that has control over our habitual behavior and controls perception. Your paradigm controls your habits, from your habits flow your productivity. I want you to remember that all behavior is habitual. In the widow's subconscious, it was ok for her to ask Elisha for aide-she justified it by reminding Elisha that her husband loved God and went to the school of prophets. Ever thought about how long it took her to build up the courage to address Elisha? She literally had to build in her mind that Elisha owed her - the debt was old and past due for the creditor to demand her sons. She built the habit of having her hand out for a hand out. The widow, even after the passing of her husband, still saw him as a crush (and everyone/everything associated with him as well.)

In the body of Christ we refer to paradigms as *strongholds* 2 Corinthians 10:4 ESV states "For the weapons of our warfare are not of the flesh but have divine power to destroy strongholds." Your belief system-established by family, community, education, created a mindset and accompanying habits (some good and some bad) towards how you approach challenges and "work." You find yourself with money management skills you have, work ethic, drive, etc. A stronghold is defined as a place that has been fortified so as to protect it against attack or a place where a particular cause or belief is strongly defended or upheld. These habits come from a belief that was founded by a lie.

The Apostle Paul tells us in Ephesians 4:23 NKJV "be renewed in the spirit of your mind." Your behavior and approach are subconscious issues; the spirits of distraction and procrastination are deeply rooted in your subconscious. The Prophet Hosea says in Hosea 4:6 NKJV "My people are destroyed for lack of knowledge. Because thou hast rejected knowledge, I will also reject thee, that thou shalt be no priest to me; because you have forgotten the law of your God, I will also forget your children." Relationship with God brings down strongholds - entrepreneurship is spiritual and is how one works, serves, and worship. Based on what you see, where you're from, and the family and friends you grew up around-it's difficult to see destiny but not so with God's grace. I'm confident that the widow became so good at using her oil she shocked everyone who knew her before becoming an entrepreneur. Let relationship and knowledge of God and His grace bring down strongholds and paradigms, let God be true and begin to work, serve, and worship. Get so good that your doubters will ask in amazement like Nathaniel in John 1:46 NKJV "can anything good come out of Ypsilanti, Michigan?" Your supporters will respond like Philip, "come and see."

You are a creative being, made in the image of God. An entrepreneur from birth but the thief comes to steal, and to kill, and to destroy John 10:10 NKJV - how does he do that? By keeping you mentally occupied elsewhere, I had to learn that. I've heard it said, "they're trying to hold me back," "they don't want me to prosper." You're right but before you challenge the natural "they" you must battle the spiritual "they" - your strongholds (or paradigms)! The enemy cannot have you to take dominion because it means he loses dominion, your oil blesses and impacts someone, and you become what God has always said about you.

This concept of paradigms is important because you attract your thoughts in accordance to the vibe you're in. Bob Proctor says "people are in a vibration that is giving results they don't want but they're comfortable in them..."

See, the awareness of your oil is a new idea, you've been under a crutch for so long, and naturally change isn't the most comfortable reality. Subconsciously, there's a fight because you've been given new, life changing information! Change your thinking and will yourself to success. Tell yourself (make a decision) "I will renew my mind and attract blessings according to my new thought process."

Lesson 4: Focus on the task at hand and the opportunity in front of you... Luke 10: 38-42 AMPC

4a: The enemy wants to steal, and to kill, and to destroy destiny, especially in its startup stage (while it's still an infant). Focus on what's important and pay close attention to the details!

CHAPTER 5

Peace by Piece: Inventory

The definition of **inventory** is a complete list of items such as property, goods in stock, or the contents of a building. **Inventory management** is the overseeing and controlling of the ordering, storage and use of components that a company will use in the production of the items it will sell as well as the overseeing and controlling of quantities of finished products for sale. There is power in product because it creates connection between business and consumer and your business gains market share.

While in a meeting in Southfield, the Founder and Broker of a real estate agency I use to be an independent contractor for said "if you have nothing to sell, you have no customers." He was speaking to the real estate agents licensed to practice through his agency. There were several transferring agents who attended the meeting in addition to, newly licensed agents (including myself and former business partner), and longtime practicing agents. As the meeting continued, the owner of a partnering title company addressed the group and his message echoed the sentiments of the original by encouraging inventory in the marketplace, especially during peak performing months. Listings - or inventory (selling) homes gives an agent leverage during negotiations, additionally the listing agent works smarter (not harder) - why? The listing agent can supply demand, market the listing, then wait for the highest and best offer- inventory is leverage-it's simply a supply and demand world.

You have to offer something - a good or a service. Always remember, if there isn't anything to offer potential customers once the attention is attained, you not only lose the opportunity to convert a contact into a client, but you also bruise your reputation and that of the brand you're building.

Inventory is knowing what you have and how much of it you have so you can measure what it will take to meet your goal, it is also knowing the cost associated with each individual component that make the sale of the whole product. In this case, oil + bottles = a bottle of oil. Every piece has a cost that dictate the setting price associated with the unit once it is in the marketplace. Your job is not to anticipate value, it's to set a market price that will allow your business to see a profit per unit.

For some entrepreneurs there's this notoriety they seek after, but this is where runners and chasers are distinguished. A runner wants the popularity to be based on them, "look at me, I have this" or "look at me, I sell this." A chaser, on the other hand, prefers to deflect attention towards the business. The product is more important than the title - without a product or service (or a product that compliments your service) there is no income, if there is no income, there is no business. Understand that? Without a product or service, you have nothing in the marketplace that is tangible to a prospective client. Runners never grasp the concept that popularity can overshadow gain. Do you remember when the Patti Labelle Sweet Potato Pies really became popular? They were being sold at large retail outlet - and the height of popularity peaked around Thanksgiving 2015. A viral video surfaced and spearheaded the craze, the person in the video became famous, was on talk shows, even Steve Harvey used the power of this personality to promote his bacon brand during a segment on his talk show featuring Patti Labelle. While watching the Patti Pie YouTube viral video we got a chance to hear an amazing voice, a great talent that just was awarded an opportunity to capitalize immensely from the traffic the viral video generated. A voice that, if coupled with a good musical sound bed could have sold records. The YouTube sensation had no inventory; no music for sale on Spotify, Amazon, Google, TIDAL, and/or iTunes, no 'I will review your product for: 15 seconds" advertisement on Fiverr, no agent or manager and incidentally became the greatest sales person for everyone but themselves. Moral of the story, the meal should be prepared before the guest arrive.

Knowing Your Numbers

Keep in mind that this chapter is not an in-depth overview about inventory. It is, however, a reflection on the importance of inventory and how it relates to goal setting using the biblical verse as a foundational overlay. Why is it so important to know your numbers? Knowing your numbers, is a two-part concept which direct towards your goals and tells you how to get there based on the material you have. Now, let's look at our chips - to be licensed as a food vendor (and distributor), we need:

1. The license
2. Insurance
3. A food safety plan (which will require a certified Preventive Controls Qualified Individual)
4. A licensed kitchen (with storage)
5. Bags (1.5 mil or greater)
6. Our products (plantain vendor and the price of oil)
7. Energy (kitchen uses gas and electric)
8. Boxes (for shipment)
9. Website (e-commerce)

I'm not scratching the surface - but imagine accounting for all these cost prior to setting a retail price that is competitive on the market place.

Jesus emphasized the importance of counting the cost of commitment Luke 14:28 ESV "For which of you, desiring to build a tower, does not first sit down and count the cost, whether he has enough to complete it?" Anxious runners go this route often, they don't want to wait and are impatient, finding themselves with an elevator pitch for an incomplete project. I encourage you to start from the end first then work your way backwards, always having extra inventory to account for unforeseen problems.

The scripture never identifies how much the woman's debt was, but it did say that if she did not pay she would lose her two sons to slavery (goal). In Zechariah 11:12-13 NIV, the value of a person was thirty pieces of silver, which Judas Iscariot received for Jesus. So, for the sake of this example, let's conclude that widowed owed sixty pieces of silver.

Thirty pieces of silver are about five weeks money (based on a six-day working week, one day's wage is called a denarius) The women were about ten weeks of pay behind on her debt. I've received those collection calls and letters that were two and a half months behind on a debt, those "if you don't make a payment now we'll have to move to our next course of action," the next course usually implies foreclosure or repossession. Nowadays companies try to work with you but at the time of this scripture I'm not convinced that they were as lenient. King Solomon tells us in Proverbs 22:7 ESV "The rich rules over the poor, and the borrower is the slave of the lender." Keep all that in mind as you imagine the journey she had to make while going to speak with the man of God. The puffy eyes from tears, the drained energy, the stench of discouragement, humiliation and failure as she attempts to appeal for a handout the Man of God responds with, "you need product, you need something to sell, what do you have that we can use that you're not using?"

This reenactment may not suffice and accurately portray the true events, but it's important to understand the instruction; let's set a goal then work backwards: I owe ten weeks of a day's wage on my mortgage, how many bottles of oil did she have to produce to meet the goal before her sons became slaves? Again, only house what you need. The Bible says once she got to the last bottle the oil stopped flowing. I would hope that her pricing strategy was aggressive - there's always a customer willing to pay for a great product no matter the cost (and this clearly isn't just regular oil.) Pricing strategy should be based on your goals and your numbers (yet competitive in the marketplace); how much for the raw material, marketing, storage, staff and delivery. Once you have those numbers, per unit, price to pay yourself back and "live off the rest." There's more that goes into inventory and I would recommend reading Max Muller's book *Essentials of Inventory Management* for a thorough analysis of the subject.

Lesson 5: Know your numbers; Luke 14:28 ESV

5a: Knowing your numbers can keep you on track to hit your goals

CHAPTER 6

Get the Jars

Romans 5:3-4 NIV reads that suffering produces perseverance; perseverance, character; and character, hope. Raising money to launch your business is character producing activity, but it requires courage and faith because unless the Lord builds the house, the builders labor in vain - Psalm 127:1 NIV. Getting the jars takes prayer, practice, and persistence - you'll be able to absorb the word "no" and convert it into fuel.

This chapter is interesting because you may have heard the widow's story preached as the Man of God encouraging the Women to use debt to finance her growth, different versions of the Bible use the word "borrow" instead of "ask" for jars - I won't argue with that teaching but I want to expand your appreciation of the verse and introduce multiple options to the funding of your business, In addition, the biblical reference, depending on where you're at in securing financing for your business, has room for potential different scenarios to get you funded. Since this section is about financing your business, it is encouraged that you communicate with a professional in your area to help you along this process. Several colleges and universities house an entrepreneurship center that can be an awesome local resource, as well as connecting with the SBA and the SBDA.

Always encouraging to develop a track record of sales and activity for funding mediums, it's not impossible to fund an idea but mostly investors fund the fire and ambition in the entrepreneur, that's why one of the first things you'll have to learn is how to develop an elevator pitch (which we'll discuss later). If you're not working your oil, then you may not completely believe in your oil, if so - why should anyone else believe in it? Expect to be (and not in all cases) prepared and be willing to give something in return (or exchange for). That something can range from shares to T-shirts and other free items. Be always mindful that this process takes work but isn't impossible - you can and will get funded with persistence and commitment.

How Much Do I Need?

Good question, right? Know your numbers (here we go again), don't guess here. God called us to operate in dominion, which is synonyms with excellence, not confusion- I remember when I was working at the bank, one of my customers was/is a restaurant entrepreneur whom I enjoyed working with - a lot, awesome personality who served great food. Their restaurant was a few minutes away from our branch, in walking distance, so my coworkers and I would eat there often. One day, staff from the restaurant came to our branch to cash their checks. They would come to my branch because I was the only Spanish speaking banker close to them who was able to communicate and help them. This day the account had negative balances and we were unable to cash their checks. I explained to the staff that they should go and consult with their manager (owner of the restaurant) but that the checks wouldn't be able to be cashed at the present moment. Of course, they had their assumptions, but I could neither confirm nor deny, later that day the owner's wife came by our branch to speak with me, with tears in her eyes she explained how they didn't have enough to pay staff, rent, order food, and everything else you could imagine. I felt horrible hearing the story, they applied for a loan and got denied. Within a couple of days, the restaurant was closed. They've since learned their lesson, they're at a new location, partnered with someone and they're doing great. Moral of the story - ambition is awesome but alone, it will not carry you, know your numbers.

I would recommend planning for at least 60 days extra in capital. A generic list of startup expenses include:

1. Research expenses - This is where you learn your industry. You can do this yourself, remember it's about activity management. If you choose to hire, you'll be paying a research firm a great deal. Cut this cost by doing the work yourself (my advice), learn your market, industry and potential customers.

2. Insurance, license and permit fees - Every industry is different, and every cost is different, research these numbers and earmark them. It would be embarrassing to acquire a building, do all repairs and not get to open because you forgot to get permits pulled. As my wife says "Ayi Yai Yai!"

3. Equipment and supplies - Again, every industry is different (as is every business), you may just need paint, a computer, phone, printer / copier, pens, paper, etc. While someone else may need a stove, oven, fryer restaurant kitchen exhaust hood and ventilation system and a POS system. Know your cost and plan accordingly, you do not want to budget for $50,000 when you really need $100,000 in startup capital.

4. Advertising and promotion - I think Facebook has a great promotional platform that enables you to connect with the people that like your product and page. Google AdWords is another great platform that helps people find you by keyword search. These are two of several platforms to consider for paid advertisement but remember, best is word of mouth, try to build organically. Snapchat can help you tell your story, as can Instagram, Facebook, Twitter and a lot of other platforms. You still may need flyers, also your signage, menu and website will be considered marketing.

5. Borrowing costs - How much is your loan and interest? What is your payment schedule, if you funded through crowdfunding you [may] not have this expense - most take a small percentage upfront, if you sold shares, your accountant can handle your dividend disbursements.

6. Employee expenses - Learn from the lesson above, keep these people happy because they will keep your customers happy and help you spread the word. How much staff do you need to run your operation? What are you going to pay each member?

7. Technological expenses - This is your internet, computer and computer repairs, phone bill and security system. Maybe you have a TV in your lobby or you use internet radio - these costs should be included also. I would also recommend you contact your energy provider and ask for a monthly quote, on average - try and price for this.

Now there are some industries with a relatively low startup cost, such as the real estate industry but you should always plan to have cash on hand because in real estate your office cost (which is like rent which (in some cases) includes broker fees (that is what your broker charges for using their name, E & O insurance, and technology combined), board fees and marketing/advertising must always be planned for.

God gave you this anointing because He knew you could handle it, but you should take it seriously and give it back to the people because anointing is transformational. I mean this from my heart you can get your business funded, do not think otherwise, do not doubt but have courage and with faith and patience it will happen. Hebrews 6:12 ESV reads "so that you may not be sluggish, but imitators of those who through faith and patience inherit the promises."

Elisha's Advice

2 Kings 4:3 NIV Elisha said, "Go around and ask all your neighbors for empty jars. Don't ask for just a few"

How do you read this, is this about debt or equity? I've primarily heard the debt interpretations of what Prophet Elisha is saying but what I can tell you is there is no one [correct] path in funding your business but it only works if you do, see the first part of the sentence? "Go around and ask all your neighbors for empty jars." That implies action, let's modernize it, "go around and ask as many banks as it takes until you get a yes" or "go online and create a Kickstarter page and share it with everyone you know until you hit your goal" or "connect with an Angel Investor and ask to pitch your idea." Bottom line, a promise is always associated with an action - God gives when you commit. You can will your way to your blessings!

Regarding the way the widow's story is taught, I believe and agree with the teaching that Elisha did encourage debt but not to hurt her more, instead it served two purposes 1. Changing her mindset 2. Expediting her launch. The one thing about debt is it's risky and requires maturity to manage but can be a tool to start your business (not my preferred method but I have seen it work great for some people).

The widow went around asking or seeking help (we know that by how she approached Elisha), additionally her neighbors, aware of what was going on at the home, may have just been providing help. This time it was different, instead of asking for help ask for the bottles and say I'll pay you back. This was a shock to her, more debt? Yet, she was obedient to the instructions - of which one was to go to all your neighbors asking them for empty jars and get, from each one, as many as you can. I want to write from three different approaches to open your mind a bit to your options; Debt perspective, Equity perspective, and Business grants.

Debt perspective

Debt is a quick solution that can provide the resources you need to jumpstart your business, but you must be responsible with the management of debt and not overwhelm yourself. Some banks love small businesses and understand that small business is the cornerstone of the local economy - those banks will lend but the business owner will be guarantor of the loan. Meaning if the business defaults, you're responsible for the loan - for this, I recommend making sure your personal credit is good. You should also be mindful of the risk. Why I love the approach Elisha took with the widow is because he challenged her mindset. She thought her credit wasn't good any longer and she wouldn't qualify, she also thought she had no way out and no way to launch. Although, I personally am not an advocate of the debt approach, I've seen it work for many and have used it myself when buying equipment and considering cash flow. I don't like debt because it enslaves but everyone's start is unique. My advice would be to pay off debts quickly, so your bottom line will increase. The widow already had the oil, just needed the packaging. Now, her debts are doubled but she was ready to sell. Remember, there's the debt that she is already behind on in addition to these bottles. "Go, sell the oil and pay your debts. You and your sons can live on what is left." Notice, "debts" is plural. The instruction appears as Elisha saying, "pay your obligations in full as soon as possible and live of the rest," nonetheless she was able to start.

Equity perspective

Equity is the value of shares issued by a company. You pay for those shares based on the valuation of the company. Have you ever watched Shark Tank? The Sharks purchase equity based on valuation. I want you to look at your business and ask yourself, "how much is it valued at?" What if I offered some people an opportunity to invest in my company and paid a dividend (if there's a gain). This is an interesting perspective and I encourage you to speak with a corporate lawyer and an accountant if you decide to pursue this route.

How to value a business:

Your business is worth whatever your think it is worth within the criteria you use to associate a number with it. As the owner, your estimation is driven by different ways to value the business and ultimately choosing the mix that reflects your final value estimate. If you're just starting out, this method of securing financing may be a bit difficult without sales volume and sweat equity but it's worth the information.

One way to look at valuation is by looking at our previous chapter - what do you have in inventory and how many assets do you own? This way is popular because you can price the company based on what's tangible - if you're in the service industry it will be based on assets and customers, methods, and intellectual property.

Another way to value is based on sales volume and industry - this is a bit more complex Warren Buffett uses the **discounted cash-flow (DCF) analysis.** DCF is a method of valuing a project, company, or asset using the concepts of the time value of money. All future cash flows are estimated and discounted by using cost of capital to give their present values (PVs).

Business Grants

You'll be surprised to learn how many grants and contest are available for college students, minority owned businesses, low income entrepreneurs, and women owned businesses. To qualify for these (some not all), you will have to become a certified minority or women owned business, but they are available because these two groups are presumed to be socially and economically disadvantaged, they have so much potential but may not have the resources to compete in the marketplace. The widow's neighbors may have saw this as an opportunity to help her - maybe they saw that she was economically disadvantaged but noticed her potential. The SBA has an 8(a) Business Development program where they help qualifying minority-owned firms develop and grow their businesses through one-to-one counseling, training workshops, and management and technical guidance. In other words, this program, like many others, are bottles waiting to be used! Her neighbors saw old useless bottles and said, "whatever you need to help you get moving."

Funding Your Anointing

I've been to seminars, I've met with "experts" and read books about funding your idea and in my experience most "experts" have read the same books I have but never had to get anything funded. You must do this yourself and truth be told, it is possible. There are so many platforms today that will help you fund your idea. Most "experts" aren't experts at all, they're opinionated employees - they haven't gone where you want to go - listen to God and follow your heart, these experts may tell you that your idea is a bad idea and it will never get funded but God has the final say, just don't be petty when they apply for a job. From experience, you're going to have to ask friends and family, research grants, apply for loans, use platforms like Kickstarter, audition for Shark Tank, and work on your elevator pitch (I recommend having more than one elevator pitch- every audience is different.) Knowledge is power, and the Prophet Elisha is helping us realize that the only thing stopping us from funding our anointing is a lack of action.

Not everyone has a millionaire friend or cousin, not all of our parents were good stewards of their finances who are able to help fund our project but to circle back to chapter 3 your network may have those resources. You may already be connected to someone, indirectly, that can help you kick start your ambition but are you prepared? Have you tried pursuing your funding first? What are your sales like now? These are questions that you may need to answer when preparing to approach someone for funding. "Poor men throw money away, rich men save, but the wealthy invest" - Dr. Myles Munroe. There are people and organizations that will fund you, but have you worked and fought before asking for help? This is a chaser's game, you may be denied 30 times before you get one yes but with faith and patience you will get funding.

Approaches to Consider

1. KickStarter (and other crowdfunding websites) - I've seen this approached effectively, what I've learned from it is that your friends are willing to help, even if by sharing the page with their sphere of influence. I ran a very selfish and unsuccessful campaign to go back to Panama for the 100-year anniversary of the Canal, I didn't incorporate everything I learned above - I just wanted to try it. I took all that I learned and coached my sister, she ran an effective GoFundMe campaign to open her daycare, very successfully. A good crowdfunding campaign has a few things:

    a. It is descriptive and provides a sense of ownership to the ones donating to your cause. People want to feel like they're a part of an important moment. Be genuine in your description and don't try and hustle people - they have better ways of investing their hard-earned money. Ex; someone wants to see you open your business because you'll be bringing jobs to the community, hiring veterans and youth. I've seen people support weddings, funerals, and college educations. Point is, when it's genuine and has a good agenda people will want to get involved.

    b. There's an incentive, ex; you provide free shirts or hats for a donation of $10 - $25, and the incentive gets better at every donation level, trick is you must transparent and reliable. Let people know who the company is and how to get in contact with you and make good on your offers. I ran a campaign and wasn't successful -

2. SBA loans - The US Small Business Administration 504 Loan or Certified Development Company program was created to provide financing for the purchase of fixed assets, which usually means real estate, buildings and machinery, at below market rates. Now here's how this works, you must go to a participating bank that works with the Agency. The Agency does not provide the money directly, the participating bank provides the SBA Financing, the SBA guarantees a percentage of those loans and the application process is long, they want to know everything. If they're going to help you get started, then put some action behind all the talk.

3. Friends and family - This is tricky, let's face it - we all have family members we love to death that will do anything for you, we also have family members that we haven't spoken with for quite some time and we also have family we hate speaking to. Doesn't matter here, those you think will help won't and those you think won't will. List them all, call them, email them, text them. General rule of thumb; three messages max - you don't want to be considered a hassle (especially if it may take you longer to launch than anticipated)

4. Competitions - This is open, typically, to minority owned businesses and college student entrepreneurs. It's usually an essay and presentation format but is a great place to look.

5. Angel Investors (elevator pitches) - Have you practiced your elevator pitch? Do you know your numbers, sales, and valuation? Angel investors have been around for years but been popular with shows like Shark Tank.

6. Self-funding (using your job as your seed) - There is absolutely nothing wrong with working a job to start your business. I have seen some people set some money aside each paycheck, allocated specifically for their oil. You can also tap into your retirement to help fund your oil - don't rush, manage your emotions and be diligent. If you don't have the means to jump

out immediately then use your job until you're ready. The key is to always do something, daily, towards your goals.

7. Selling / flipping - When we first got started, we were catering than taking some of that money, buying more supplies, paying off certain goals, until we could get launched. As a matter of fact, we paid for logos and trademarks by selling tamales and tacos. There's always something you can flip, if you work on cars offer the cheap oil changes in your neighborhood until you can pay off your license fees or get a garage. Same goes with any other business, treat it like a barter system - how I got started with DreamYpsi is we would offer free artwork in exchange for a client referral. Flip your way to the top.

8. Partnerships - Key here is to partner with someone who has something you do not have. Let's say you want to open a lawn care business, you have the truck and friends with houses that need affordable lawn care, but you do not have the lawnmower, partner with someone who can strengthen your weakness. Now apply that to money - you have the idea, passion, work-ethic and knowhow but not the money. Here's what you do, always retain a higher share of the company but say let's do a 55/45 split (or better), you fund me, I'll work you get paid. You can always buy the person out of their contract later (or keep them if it's working well).

9. Selling your home (home equity lines of credit) - Although I'm not a fan of selling your home, I've have colleagues and friends that tapped into the equity of their home from the sale or a HELOC (home equity line of credit). This is a unique approach but be mindful because most HELOCs are a variable rate which increase with Prime. HELOCs are usually reserved for repairs, improvements or consolidation of debts. With this loan you only pay what you use plus the interest, you don't pay on the entire amount (unless you use it).

10. Use a credit card - Not a fan here because credit card interest rates are high and are variable - meaning as Prime increases

so do these rates. But you know what's best for you and your family. Again, I'm not the biggest fan of debt because of its risk but if you're mature enough to manage it then go forward.

11. Get a Microloan - Microloans are small loans I believe it's typically between $500 - $50,000 (maybe) $100,000 depending on the institution. To qualify for this loan, you must have up to five (5) employees and up to $50,000 in capital needs. You can pretty much use these loans for anything. Speak to your local banker for more information.

What We Did

We sold tamales, used our jobs - savings, paychecks, and retirement, and applied for grants such as Motor City Match, HATCH Detroit, and The Awesome Foundation. Our first location was our house, then we moved to a kitchen we rented from a church. This approach was most affordable for us and allowed us to grow one customer at a time. I maintained my job and used our income as our launchpad, my wife managed and trained for the FSPCA and ServSafe, working alone many times while I attended classes for certifications or stayed in the library writing our business plans, or designing our label/menu or website.

I wanted to share because not everyone's story is the same and to be honest you shouldn't hope that it is. Your story is what makes your venture unique and that uniqueness is what gravitates people towards you. Be unashamed here, we sold tamales, arroz con pollo, flute tacos, tres leche cakes, pupusas, cheese cake, cilantro lime chicken, empanadas, and baleadas to raise money because that's what we knew how to do.

Lesson 6: Embrace your journey. Your journey is more important than the mountain peak

6a: Regardless of what options are available, if you're not active there's no purpose in knowing them.

CHAPTER 7

Open Your Door

*She went and told the man of God, and he said, "**Go,
sell the oil and pay your debts. You and your sons
can live on what is left.**" (Emphasis added)*

2 Kings 4:7 NIV

You've worked hard - now let's jump. According to Revelations 21:8 NLT, cowards will be grouped with those who practice witchcraft, are idol worshippers, and liars:

"But cowards, unbelievers, the corrupt, murderers, the immoral, those who practice witchcraft, idol worshipers, and all liars--their fate is in the fiery lake of burning sulfur. This is the second death."

We tend to skip steps or skim instruction manuals, just to get going - sometimes I get it, you never know if you're ready till you jump and I've been guilty of it. For example, I've never read a car's manual until I needed a repair and I regularly skim through assembly manuals just to find myself spending more time than I needed to assemble an entertainment center. It's a part of our fallen nature, Adam and

Eve skipped an instruction also. Although this isn't a book on the psychology of the human nature, it is important to note that the widow's commitment to instruction yielded her desired result (and more than she could ask or think). We cannot skip process, we must go through law school to become a lawyer, and you must be licensed to sell food and so on so forth. The Man of God was detailed in his instruction, which she obeyed, and now she's selling.

Before Peter could walk on water in Matthew 14:28, and before Peter's shadow could heal in Acts 5:15, Peter had to become a fisher of men, Matthew 4:19 ESV reads "And he said them, "Follow me, and I will make you fishers of men." This rule should apply in and outside of the church - before your guest arrive cook your food. I've learned that dedication comes before proclamation - spend some time researching your consumer behavior patterns (or hire a team to help you with market research), understand the potential impact of digital marketing - take ownership of the process, or hire someone to manage your digital performance. Additionally, spend some time learning local organic platforms that will help you draw attention to your business - like local news outlets.

You got your inventory (product) and you figured out your cash flow, it's time to sell (distribute). View this section as your grand opening, be mindful, just because you slap an open sign on your door doesn't guarantee any customers. You must have a product to advertise than you must advertise, telling your target audience about your product(s) and/or service(s) then you must monitor what you manage, keep a record of your current clients and new prospects (custom audience and lookalike audience). This type of organization enables you to tailor your marketing message to fit each client at their point of interaction with your business. Communication helps you to know your customer, know your goals and exceed your goals.

Marketing is the part of the vision which encourages an action; sale, download, sign-up for a newsletter, etc. Beyond marketing, there are several influencing components that drive the potential of customer conversion; on your website - is the product within three clicks and is there transparency about your business to your customers? Answering these questions creates a positive user experience and increases the likelihood of a conversion. In person, is the deal valuable? Can I get it elsewhere? If so, is it cheaper? How's my interaction with the sales person? Was the salesperson personable or pushy? Do I need it? Think of your customer while marketing, as a matter of fact think of yourself as a customer while marketing your product. How do you respond to pushy sales people? What's more important to you, convenience or a sale? What benefits are you looking for from a product?

The Man of God said, "open the door"—p go work, get active and be passionate, all the steps prior to opening the door prepared you for sales; you identified your product, have a packaged product (inventory), know how many you need to sell to breakeven and to be in the black (know your numbers), now all that's left to do is to hit your numbers. There's a target audience created specifically for your product, I really believe that there's always a customer (target audience) that will purchase your product, but you must be prepared for the sale. Know your scripts and get ready to sell.

Production & Trade

Have you noticed the transition she's gone through in seven verses? Started off with entitlement ended with a business. Do you really believe people have to support your effort because you're open or because they're family/friends? The adage "build it they will come" will leave you with an empty building, go beyond your warm market and I understand the mistake of the assumption but money is a sensitive topic, for it to exchange hands it has to be trustworthy transaction in which the consumer feels that they will get something in return of value. In house support isn't sustainable for growth, you'll have to branch out of your comfort zone for the results you're looking for.

We started serving food in October of 2012 out of our home kitchen, our first clients were our warm market (family and friends), for a while we could count on them and then the inevitable happened - they said "no." Either the "no" was due to budget or the "no" was due to ease of access, at the end of the day the "no" changed the way we approached word of mouth. I learned that I'm not entitled to your support, the promise wasn't in the handout, it was in the hustle.

Have you ever been too broke to pay your bills, isn't your hustle a bit different? When we're comfortable we approach obstacles from the perspective of our comfort, but when the rent is due and we're short we approach hustle from the perspective of survival. Comfort has killed abundance many times, and I believe comfort was one of the stones that killed Goliath comfort makes you act like you've arrived, but the survival mindset keeps you working [hard] well after your rent is paid and you're out of the red.

The Man of God challenged her perspective and flipped the switch in her mind that shifted her from a comfortable handout receiver to a hustler. I've been on WIC and Bridge Cards (EBT), I hated being on them and was embarrassed pulling them out at the checkout line, trying to hide it behind other cards. I also realized that while using government assistance, I knew I could count on my food budget being met so I didn't hustle the money was already there. I didn't have to survive and figure out how to pay the bills and feed my family until I stopped accepting assistance. At that point I remembered to pray than act, we didn't need "assistance" we needed a reality check.

Since the beginning, God established business and desired entrepreneurs to produce and trade upon ethical standards; advancing the Kingdom, helping the poor, widow and orphan, providing employment opportunities and paying taxes. In Old Testament economies curses and blessings were partially established by your business principles and ethics; Proverbs 11:26 ESV reads the people curse him who holds back grain, but a blessing is on the head of him who sells it. The expectation God has for your business is for you to hustle, not receive a handout. Produce and sell, not promote while procrastinating.

Positioning, Packaging, Pricing, Promotions

Marketing and sales are exact complements. They work together to drive the desired result, a customer conversion. Marketing isn't as simple as it looks neither is it as complicated as I'm making it appear. It does, although, require ambition and strategy. People tend to support, do business with and purchase from what they've seen most and have been considered a reliable and trusted product. Per usual, about 5 - 7 views encourage an action. In other words, a customer is influenced to act upon (your desired course of action) by consistent visibility of a product that produces a benefit they are seeking. When you're in the grocery store and in the market for a soda, will you purchase a Coke or an RC Cola? Let's assume both products are on sale for the same price and positioned at eye level aisle end caps facing the front of the grocery store towards the cash registers across from the tortilla chips. Yet, you've tasted Coke already (and you're familiar with it), also, you've seen more promotions for Coke; online, in your favorite magazine, TV and radio. Will you purchase RC Cola? Of course, if you prefer the taste you will but for the casual consumer Coke will get their dollar.

I define marketing as the positioning, packaging, pricing and promotions a business prioritizes for their product to be successful in today's market landscape which drives customer conversion. Customer conversion is defined as the desired result at the end of a customer's interaction with your product or service. Let's assume you have a blog and your goal is for users to download an article; the more your blog post (which has the downloadable material) is seen by users - whether on social media and/or paid advertisement, the likelihood of a download is increased. Seems like common sense, correct? Yet many entrepreneurs only tag their friends' social media walls and post on their own social media pages, are these people even paying attention to you? Who is your target audience? Dig a different well, the internet has created a platform for you to distribute, the traditional ways are still resourceful, but you must get it out there, so you can get your product or service in front of people you haven't met yet.

Positioning

It's natural that you want to place your product on a platform that can generate the most traffic possible, while this is desired, most entrepreneurs (initially) don't have the resources to accomplish this goal but that's not to say that you can't capitalize where your budget or your partnerships allow. With tools, online, such as Facebook Ads, Bing and Google AdWords you can have great placement on searches most relevant to your product or on pages of people who have interest in what you offer. Afterwards, go back to your network and ask them if they know buyers in retail (that can get your product in stores), bloggers or columnist who can review your product and publish their feedback. Aim for traffic, the goal with positioning is to be on platforms that will generate discovery. In some cases, there are cost associations with great positioning, but the results introduce your product to people who haven't seen it yet. Now remember, there's the 5 - 7 rule, consumers want to see consistency and will have had to have seen (or heard) about your product 5 - 7 times before they consider a purchase. My mentor used to call this the BBD (bigger better deal), he associated marketing to the psychology of the consumer and said the more people see your product positioned in high traffic places with great artwork, the consumer will assume that you have the "bigger better deal" and they want to do business with you. I want to add to that theory that the product must be a good product because the online distribution platforms also allow for customer reviews, be mindful that reviews can negatively impact your sales or positively impact your sales.

Packaging

I'm a huge fan of packaging, so much so that I won't purchase a good product if the packaging is bad. Growing up, I use to go a barber shop in Ann Arbor and when there was a new barber no one would go to them, the joke used to be "if the haircut is bad but the hairline is good you may be able to get away with it until it grows back." I still laugh when I think about it because it's so true, have you ever gone to a movie that was packaged so well that you just knew "this has to be great" only to find yourself falling asleep halfway through the movie? Packaging is everything and even extends to customer service. I've gone to restaurants because the artwork was good, menu items looked great, site was clean, great reviews on food, but the customer service didn't match the packaging and I never came back.

Packaging is important because it allows you to stand out, it allows you look like the BBD. When you're first starting out you won't be able to afford being as fancy as your major competitors and that shouldn't deter you, a runner will abandon because they cannot compete while a chaser will procrastinate because they can't afford. Find the good! Although you may not have the perfect package you can compete by having a clean look, a nice sticker label, use WordPress to build your site, etc. Once money comes in, reinvest (eventually) in packaging but make changes when necessary. Never rush to compete with packaging just do what you can and redefine packaging. Remember my restaurant analogy above? Get the best pictures you can afford, keep your food fresh and establishment clean but focus on customer service and you will outperform your competition. Great tasting food is awesome but great experience is everything. Your restaurant will be remembered because of its entire package.

Pricing

How much does it cost to make your product? How much are competitors selling theirs for? How much should you sell yours for? What's your average ticket and how many units do you have to sell at that average; per week, month, and year, to break even or go black? This is pricing, when we're first starting out entrepreneurs are so eager to get out there they price their product at an introductory level, unknowingly barely making any money because it cost much more to produce than they anticipated. This woman had several loans now, the bottles and the debt her husband left behind - her pricing for each bottle had to be just right for her to hit numbers and her pricing fluctuated. Since she was "borrowing" bottles from all her neighbors, it's safe to assume not all bottles were the same size. Some bottles may have been sold for more than others. Maybe you have different product lines within the same product that have different price associations per unit; like a phone with an 8gb, 16gb and 32gb variation - overall you will look at the overall sale of your product by classifying each different variation. For example; I sold 100 units of phone X; 8 GB sold 23 units at $199 each unit, 16 GB sold for $299 each unit and we sold 34 units and our 32 GB sold 43 units at $399 each unit.

Your price will also influence if someone is willing to buy, pricing too high you'll never sell while pricing too low you can lose consumer trust. Price with a goal in mind (conversion), learn the trend and try to stay consistent within it.

Promotions

Who doesn't like a good promotion? A good promotion is mutually beneficial for consumer and business. It allows you to introduce your product to more consumers while allowing your consumer to save a bit of money. It's a great way to start and a great way to push sales when you're starting to slow down. Promotions keep you current in front of demand.

Targeting

Targeting is defined as identifying your audience and creating marketing messages tailored to that group. You can target by region, race, gender, age anything you can think of. After you identify which group you want to target and you create effective messages for them that influence them to visit your store or consider your product (or service), you can create a sub-message that influence a return visit or completes a transaction. This is called re-targeting. Re-targeting is how you find out your customers behavior pattern; where they shop, what other pages they visit online or where they like to go offline, your goal with re-targeting is to stay within the 5-7 rule, you want to limit the exposure to 30 days, otherwise you become overbearing, but 4 weeks is usually sufficient.

Sub-messages are in the background and echo your original message with a slightly different call to action. Online you can do this by tracking cookies, offline this is done by extensive research of your target audience. For example, let's say you make an appealing ad on Facebook or Google AdWords and users click on your ad which directs them to your website. While on your website (you must be transparent) tell your visitors that you track cookies, let's assume they don't make a purchase, this is where your sub-message kicks in. Your cookies discovery that the user likes to visit blogs or site that sell men's apparel, if that site uses Google AdSense, Google will add your sub-message in the ad space available. The message should now discreetly encourage the finish of a transaction. While Facebook will submit your ad on their timeline (even if they don't 'like' your business page.

Targeting is a powerful tool, get in the habit of knowing the type and behavior of the person who buys your product or tries your service.

It's not enough to assume "everyone" will like my product—runners assume that and find it to be a frustrating path towards revelation that no, not everyone likes your product!

Sell with Strategy

Targeting is important because it allows you to identify who does like your product or service, you know this because the potential client either visited your site or made a purchase from you. What about the potential consumers who may like your product but haven't heard of you yet? Selling with a strategy is about tracking down your customers and tailoring messages that appeal to those who have interacted with you and those who haven't heard about you.

Never approach anything without a strategy. The best way to meet someone who hasn't heard of you yet is through cold calling, best times to call are from 9am - 11am and 4pm - 5pm (why?) Let's face it, at 9am our work day is just starting, and we're alert. At 4pm our day s ending and we're on our phones scrolling. Consistency is key here, not every day but once a week check in until you can set up a meeting, visit in store or a request for 'do not call'. Online this is accomplished by your social media paid advertisements. Facebook is good at attracting the people who haven't heard about you.

My second favorite approach to meet people who haven't heard about my products or service is through mailers. Send mailers to your customers neighbors once a month. Imagine your customer unloading their car with one of your bags in hand and their neighbor sees it, looks in their mailbox and gets an invite to try your product. This makes a powerful impact.

Other approaches that I like are speaking opportunities, selling your product at events where you can talk about your product, or sponsoring an event (maybe giving out something free or paying for the uniforms).

This is a great way for people to hear the passion, learn about the product, see the company logo, or try the product.

Selling with a strategy means I will attempt to introduce, get to know and communicate with my clientele. It is absolutely a tragedy to not have a strategy. You're as good as your last sale.

Inspect what you Expect

I learned this concept while working for a communications company in Ann Arbor, the philosophy was simple, don't micromanage people, micromanage process. Truthfully, you can train someone to perform well in any given task, but you must manage the task to yield the results you're looking for. Thus, if you hire a sales team and assign them to make calls all day, you must provide them with a script, tools and sales tips to maximize their time and get you a lot of leads. Otherwise they'll be wasting their time and your time. This is the same across all areas of your business—inspect what you expect, or, manage the process until it yields the results you're looking for.

I've come to believe that people are only efficient if the process is explained well and they have access to the tools required for the expected results. Stop blaming your staff for your poor implementation of your vision.

The widow followed her instructions to the tee she succeeded, furthermore, Elisha gave her clear instructions, there was no grey area. Also, after every step, she checked back. Elisha was able to inspect what he expected he knew the process worked. She executed and was able to sell her product. Marketing and sales is about making sure there is an effective process that encourages customer conversion.

Open the door with a smile on your face

There's so much excitement when you're unveiling an idea and concept for sale but excitement without goals can lead to frustration. Attempt to couple your excitement with goals to constantly challenge yourself. When introducing your oil there's this feeling of 'man my life is about to change' and that's a good thing but what Elisha was teaching her was she had enough product to meet her goal, but the intensity must be the same on day 100 as it was on day 1 (so she can live off the rest). I told my business colleague "the beauty of taking your time to ensure all things are correct is that it makes room for an exciting reveal." With so many distribution platforms available online you have options, maximize your options. Remember, this is a chaser's game. A runner will get excited to reveal but not have goals so once they're not selling as many units as they had before they get discouraged and quit. A chaser, on the other hand, realizes that each distribution opportunity is a potential win to get in front of a bigger audience than before. Now we have Amazon, Google Play, iTunes, Facebook, and other distributors offline such as retail outlets Costco, Sam's Club, Walmart, etc....There are also local events you can get a booth at and sell your product(s). Remember, relationships are an important part to unlocking the door and getting prime product placement with some of your distribution partners.

When your customer comes, keep a smile on your face and offer great service from the moment they walk in (or log on) to the moment they leave (checkout), service is where it matters - quick, efficient service with a smile. Ask your customers if they liked your service and if so ask them to review you on Yelp or Google My Business, if not, fix it - leave no room for them to leave and give you a poor review. If it's an online transaction allow them to complain to you via email, offer a discount and free shipping.

Open the door, your life is about to change!

Lesson 7: Whatever you do, work at it with all your heart, as working for the Lord, not for human masters. Colossians 3:23 NIV

7a: Never, for once, lose sight of the goal or focus on anyone else. Conversions (sales, downloads, sign-ups) change things, repeat the process and stay focused!

CHAPTER 8

Invest in People

My first mentor came in early adulthood (early-mid 20's) and he would have to scrape layers of misinformation off me before he could actually teach me anything. As a matter of fact, I am (and you are) a product of the five most important voices in our lives.

Life repeats a lesson until the lesson is learned or the information is changed, then your test becomes your testimony. As the same with entrepreneurship. In Chapter 2 you found a mentor, but in Chapter 8 you will become a mentor.

2 Timothy 2:2 ESV "And what you have heard from me in the presence of many witnesses entrust to faithful men who will be able to teach others also." Paul and Timothy's relationship (or Moses and Joshua, Elijah and Elisha, Jesus and Peter) is what I like to call transformational leadership—where the elder leader was impactful in the life of the younger leader leaving a legacy of expected behavior that encouraged success. With every generation those same rules apply yet evolve to fit the current atmosphere of leadership.

Becoming a mentor involves two key stages: parenting and trailblazing. Mentorship impacts nations and improves generations. You can shape and develop young minds and help them avoid the pit stop and headaches that prolonged your oil from manifestation.

Parenting 1 Timothy 1:2 ESV - "To Timothy, my true child in the faith…"

This is taking interest and bonding with your mentee, remember how your mentor got to know you? You can't develop what you won't discover. I'm a father of four young men, although they are brothers growing up in the same household they each have their own personalities and taste. Spending time with them and learning their likes and dislikes allows me to coach them through obstacles and success in a way they will learn from.

There are some similarities you'll have, especially in business, for example the first time hearing "no" to funding or dealing with firing someone, splitting a partnership and hiring the right accountant. Or coaching through successes such as their first major contract and their first hire. Only coach on what you have the capacity to speak about and to do so you must develop a [genuine] relationship with your mentee so you can pour insight and they'll receive.

Trailblazing 1 Corinthians 11:1 ESV - "Be imitators of me, as I am of Christ."

Be an example of what to strive towards. Mentorship is responsibility and should be transparent. People 'like' the hype but follow the consistency. Allow your smile and scars to validate your experience. You may not have all the answers, but you do have an experience that worked for you. Your mentee needs your experience, they'll take your advice and adapt it to fit their need. Remember, your mentee follows what you don't say more than what you do say.

Success with Successors

On Facebook, I was tagged to a video of Dr. Myles Munroe where he states that "there is no success without a successor." Moses had Joshua, David had Solomon, and Jesus had his disciples. Your oils longevity is dependent on your ability to demonstrate, develop and deploy your successor (in part, this is like planning an exit strategy). Leaders produce leaders, no coincidence the higher you rise the air gets thinner, only a few can handle pressure. Your job is to find, coach, and develop potential and to do so search the heart not the appearance, for out of the heart character flows.

Entrepreneurship is a chaser's game, your oil (anointing) can be a tangible and profitable business with the potential to take care of several generations. Developing next generation leadership is a God inspired practice in operation with Fortune 500 companies around the world. This is how Disney, Ford, Apple and Chic Fil A thrived for decades—remember to coach up and not coach out.

I believe the instruction of closing the door "behind you and your sons" given by Elisha to the widow was for the benefit of her two sons to adjust their minds as well and allow for them to experience the sacrifice and construction of tapping into their oil. These two young men learned how to avoid the trap of what many millennials are struggling with today, producing someone else's oil for fear of producing your own. This lesson enables the young men to never repeat the cycle of their father and potentially run a successful oil company.

The widow was able to show her sons that obedience is better than sacrifice, she was able to encourage, employ, explain and empower her sons through action and obedience. She, before their very eyes, evolved from discouraged and disenfranchised to a developer of an oil distribution center. The young men witnessed the entire growth process from asking the Man of God for a handout and leaving his presence with a business, to helping her ask for bottles, helping her fill the bottles, and then helping her sell the bottles. Lastly, they witnessed her pay off the debtor and live debt free.

It was her responsibility along the way to share with her successors why there was a struggle, how God was going to give them victory by obedience to the steps outlined by the Man of God and why it was important to have faith despite the obvious fear that could have destroyed their family and their potential.

To ensure generational upward mobility, you must be willing to find someone to impart to. Be prayerful and patient, it may feel like there is no one available - I imagine that's how Samuel felt while trying to anoint Jesse's sons. Leadership development is like insuring generational success, consider Joshua's story, a young man becoming leader, applying what his mentor invested in him and ushering a new era, listening and spending time with God. Joshua was a great successor shared similar moments as Moses but experienced obvious differences. The Bible states in Joshua 5:12 NIV that "the manna stopped the day after they ate this food from the land, there was no longer any manna for the Israelites, but that year they ate the produce of the Canaan." The group Joshua lead was the generation of the children whose parents died in the wilderness. They lived through part of the wilderness experience and heard of what God did in Egypt but because the Moses era ended this group had to go about acquisition and growth differently. God was still with them, but God's approach was different for them also, read Joshua 3 in how they crossed the Jordan. Joshua had a water experience like Moses did but instead of the water splitting, they had to get wet first then it became dry as they continued walking.

Here's where Joshua was unsuccessful, he didn't invest, impart, or mentor a single person. Instead, after Joshua died in Judges 2:10-12 ESV we see that "there arose another generation after them who did not know the Lord or the work that he had done for Israel." Teach your mentee that they must mentor also and teach the lessons of what it took for the company to get where it is today, what the plans are, and what steps the company is taking to ensure fruition, which intellectual properties to pursue, trends to avoid, invest in and trends to initiate. You do this so each generation (or era of the company) can be better than the previous.

Most millennials are forced to break generational curses our parents could have for several reasons but mostly in part to the lack of fathers in the household and a poor comprehension of financial literacy. We aren't educated about entrepreneurship in our community, finance and its impact to our community, generational wealth and its impact to our community, the dollar life cycle, gentrification, ownership, etc... Information is monumental for building leaders; in business and the community. It is absolutely my responsibility to teach my children about God, faith, entrepreneurship, wealth, how to handle failure, and how to love their wives and not abandon their families - the school system won't teach them, some churches may not know how to teach them, and the media will destroy them. Learn from Joshua's error, develop, mentor and deploy so the next generation can influence culture and not be influenced by the culture.

Advance the World

Small businesses are great for the economy. In the U.S. alone, small businesses account for 46% of the nonfarm GDP. GDP is an economic term which is an abbreviation of Gross Domestic Product. So, my statement above means that small businesses make up 46% of the market value of the goods and services produced in the United States. If no one has told you that your idea is important lately, allow me to be the first.

How do you advance the world? Hiring, mentoring and developing your team to become the leaders of tomorrow in the marketplace. Grow from within, teach them what you've learned, place people correctly, give them responsibilities that stretch their comfort zones and press their oil, thereby encouraging them to face their tasks according to their unique anointing.

Lesson 8: Give instruction to a wise man, and he will be still wiser; teach a righteous man, and he will increase in learning. Proverbs 9:9 ESV

8a: Sharing is caring, pull someone else up, and change their life as someone did with you, by helping them not fail where you did!

CHAPTER 9

God and Entrepreneurship

I believe that God has a plan to prosper you and that you're about to launch one of the greatest ideas the world has ever seen and desperately needs. Do you believe this? You have a powerful anointing on you, an oil that, if pressed, can produce much. Don't be anyone else but yourself, we need you and God needs to use you. Few more things I want you to note, inactivity is the cause that kills promise, remove mental limitations, and never confuse movement with progress.

Death belongs to the fruitless

On the following day, when they came from Bethany, he was hungry. And seeing in the distance a fig tree in leaf, he went to see if he could find anything on it. When he came to it, he found nothing but leaves, for it was not the season for figs. And he said to it, "May no one ever eat fruit from you again." And his disciples heard it. Mark 11:12-14 ESV

The principle of reaping and sowing is applicable in activity versus inactivity. Change occurs through movement because resources are attracted to movement. It is unlike God to honor an idea not powered by action, but it is much like the [average thinking] man to find pride and excitement simply in a concept. The above average [thinking] man is motivated by the production of a distributed product. Inactivity does not grant you favor while on your entrepreneurial journey, it's the complete opposite. Inactivity only promises a dry season.

Since Genesis 1 God's sentiment has been to produce something and to be presently active throughout the creation process, God encouraged Adam (and all of us) to "be fruitful and multiply," he even placed Adam in the garden to "work." As mentioned throughout this book, you already have the tools—the only challenge you may encounter is the identification of your oil, but I can certainly and emphatically say that once you discover your oil, everything else will make perfect sense and all that's left is discipline.

Eliminate your limits

Romans 12:2 ESV reads; "Do not be conformed to this world, but be transformed by the renewal of your mind, that by testing you may discern what is the will of God, what is good and acceptable and perfect." This is one of my favorite verses, God is challenging believers to use His lens on our circumstance and to change how we filter thoughts and rationalize ideas. How do you view your business? What are your biggest challenges or limitations? Change how you view them - the world says you need a lot of money to get started but God says you already have access to it, just get started and the money will find you. I believe the Apostle Paul was encouraging us to approach life from the perspective that "God will supply every need of yours according to his riches in glory in Christ Jesus." Philippians 4:19 ESV. The bible tells us that God gives us the ability to create wealth - look no further than Jacob and Laban. God has the ability to give you an idea that will change your future - within your area of gifting.

In the book of Numbers chapter 13 Moses sends twelve spies into Canaan to report what the promise land looked like. If the people occupying the land were strong or weak, if there was a lot of people or just a few, if the land was rich or poor, if there were trees, the land was

Millennial Kingdom Entrepreneur

good or bad, and if the people lived in camps or strongholds. Ten of the spies reported to Moses, Aaron and the entire congregation motivated by fear based on what they saw, on the other hand; Joshua and Caleb reported with optimism and confidence inspired by the strength God showed them He could perform and said, "don't rebel, this is a good opportunity" Numbers 14:7-9 NIV. How you view something determines your pursuit of it, if the task seems too large to be victorious in, your approach is hesitant but if you know the God you serve is backing you, you make it happen!

When my sister was opening her daycare center, we had a family member offer to fund the project. My sister had such a confidence, she felt like she could do anything, she was planning this illustrious idea for her daycare. She met with the landlord and signed the lease, met with the township and got approval. She had no mental barriers because her idea was confirmed by the financial support of our cousin. That is until our cousin backed out and she had signed documents approved to open her daycare, she had to make something happen and realign her trust with the size of her God. She wanted to quit a million times, but whose report would she believe?

God cannot bless intentions or inaction and inaction is a disease caused by fear and doubt. Fear and doubt have killed more businesses than lack of finances has.

Urgency Is *Not* a Sin

Simply put, urgency doesn't mean rushing. Urgency means an excitement to release the best product you can produce in a timely manner (giving your personal circumstances). If you have not been successful at getting financed or you choose to self-finance using your savings, or Kickstarter, it may take you a bit longer than others. Be aware of the amount of time needed and budget your cost, pick a release date and be faithful to that date by releasing the best product you can

y

91

produce. We need a chaser's urgency, because although we're waiting on you, we're still waiting on the best of you. We're waiting on God's anointing to flow through you.

Urgency can be defined as excitement to supply a demand and exceed expectations in a realistic time frame. I want you to be great, active and prepared for the demand ahead of you.

Lesson 9: God's plan for you is to prosper but he'll also dry up the fruitless tree Mark 11:12-14 ESV

9a: Never think for a minute that God is not in the blessing business, problem is God can only support what you've been anointed to produce!

CHAPTER 10

Millennial Entrepreneurship: An Equally Important Part of The Body

There is one body. But it has many parts. Even though it has many parts, they make up one body. It is the same with Christ...

The body is not made up of just one part. It has many parts.

1 Corinthians 12:12, 14 NIRV

The creative impulse of entrepreneurship is exactly who you are. You were designed by a creator in His image and likeness and giving dominion over the tools you need to produce your anointing and share it with the world around you. You were born an entrepreneur but somewhere along the way you misplaced your oil, or you've set it aside while using the crutch of a spouse, parent, government assistance, or an employer - and you feel helpless and bored. There's a deep conviction and you know that you're not at your potential or even doing what you love, you can change that. You're a millennial entrepreneur living in the generation with the most access to information the world has ever seen, and you can connect with anyone around the world in the palm of your hand. Your anointing, if cultivated, will produce and release at the right time - but you must allow it to come out of you. We're in a generation whose distribution platform(s) are accessible and perform better than any generation before us - if you're a musician upload it on Sound Cloud, if you're a reseller buy it from eBay or Alibaba and sell it on Amazon, if you're a baker sell your food at a farmers market, a marketer promote yourself on LinkedIn or Fiverr - no excuses.

It is your responsibility to be faithful to the cultivation of your anointing; focus on your oil, press your oil, not the oil of others but it is acceptable to use your gift under another's anointing such as a sales person working at a bank or insurance agency, or a mechanic working at Ford, or a food entrepreneur franchising a restaurant - the goal is to use the gift and leverage whatever opportunity you have.

In a world of validation and cloning it's more difficult to identify our anointing, we are so enamored with the lives of the people we follow we've become distracted and don't properly manage our activities. In doing so, we struggle with the "be fruitful and multiply" part, that is why millennial entrepreneurship is a gift and a responsibility, we have all the tools we need to share and distribute our anointing but some millennial entrepreneurs don't succeed at two things our predecessors have succeeded with; the identification of our anointing and the production of our oil.

I'm unsure if we've substituted accessibility with work effort. That's why this book was written, to encourage you to keep fighting. Our predecessors, adversely, understood the importance of being unique and working hard but didn't have the platforms that we do—it is for that reason, to some, we're considered a lazy and rebellious generation. I don't believe millennial entrepreneurs understand the access they possess. Yet, don't be discouraged—pray and ask God to help you identify your oil and how to cultivate it. Let the Lord know you'll take a chaser's approach and you'll submit your ways to Him.

Faith

All successful people have faith, otherwise you'd go crazy. Faith sustains you to believe in the finished product despite how everything around you appear, but your faith needs to be coupled with action. "What good is it, my brothers, if someone says he has faith but does not have works? Can that faith save him?" James 2:14 ESV. Entrepreneurs may seem crazy, but it's okay... you've got to have crazy faith to get to where you're going. By faith, we become the product of our desire to produce an oil that will be used in our lamps as we shine bright for the world to witness. You have access and the same 24 hours as the person you admire most— began to use them diligently and move by faith powered by action. The reality is as a millennial entrepreneur you have the tools to become your potential, but you must manage them effectively.

Law of Loss

Effectively managing the identification of your anointing, cultivation of your anointing, production and distribution of your anointing will open opportunities for you to tap into other things you're good at also. The law of loss is a universal law about mismanagement. The law states that loss occurs due to improper management, or whatever you mismanage can no longer be in your possession. Apply the principle in any area; relationships, activity management and time, finances, health, and your business. Time is impacted by this law in concordance with how you approach activity management. Here's an example, let's assume you allot three hours of your 24 hours daily to the pursuit or improvement of your business but you miss prioritize your activities within the allotted time by watching TV or scrolling on Instagram, you will miss out on the block of advancement and negatively affect your business - nothing gets done and you're delayed another day. Looking at the law regarding finance, money is loss when the budget isn't balanced, you're not saving, and giving and you're not involved in revenue producing activities - there is no management in your finances which leaves you constantly broke and unable to invest in your anointing. In business, if you do not manage your anointing, cultivating it and constantly stretching it, taking on projects that challenge you, surrounding yourself with mentors, and support, etc..., chances are you're mismanaging the business and eventually it will suffocate from the mismanagement and fold. This is a powerful law for every millennial to understand, not just entrepreneurs, mismanagement will bring you loss.

The law is derived from the recognition that the "the earth is the LORD's and the fullness thereof, the world and those who dwell therein" Psalms 24:1 ESV. You're saying, *nothing is mines I just manage it.* Once we understand that nothing belongs to us; not our material possessions, relationships, and our families for that matter - we'll treat it differently. Imagine if you will, you're currently working at a company as a manager. Depending how you execute your task you will get promoted, demoted or fired. Same rules apply here, if I manage the few clients I have well, the owner of the company, God, will give me more clients. In finance, if I manage the little money I have well, the owner (God) will entrust me with more money.

Jesus explains this law in Luke 16:10-13 ESV

> "One who is faithful in a very little is also faithful in much, and one who is dishonest in a very little is also dishonest in much. If then you have not been faithful in the unrighteous wealth, who will entrust to you the true riches? And if you have not been faithful in that which is another's, who will give you that which is your own?

And again, in Matthew 25:14-30 NIV

> "Again, it will be like a man going on a journey, who called his servants and entrusted his wealth to them.

To one he gave five bags of gold, to another two bags, and to another one bag, each according to his ability. Then he went on his journey. The man who had received five bags of gold went at once and put his money to work and gained five bags more. So also, the one with two bags of gold gained two more. But the man who had received one bag went off, dug a hole in the ground and hid his master's money.

"After a long time, the master of those servants returned and settled accounts with them. The man who had received five bags of gold brought the other five. 'Master,' he said, 'you entrusted me with five bags of gold. See, I have gained five more.'

"His master replied, 'Well done, good and faithful servant! You have been faithful with a few things; I will put you in charge of many things. Come and share your master's happiness!'

"The man with two bags of gold also came. 'Master,' he said, 'you entrusted me with two bags of gold; see, I have gained two more.'

"His master replied, 'Well done, good and faithful servant! You have been faithful with a few things; I will put you in charge of many things. Come and share your master's happiness!'

"Then the man who had received one bag of gold came. 'Master,' he said, 'I knew that you are a hard man, harvesting where you have not sown and gathering where you have not scattered seed. So, I was afraid and went out and hid your gold in the ground. See, here is what belongs to you."

"His master replied, 'You wicked, lazy servant! So you knew that I harvest where I have not sown and gather where I have not scattered seed? Well then, you should have put my money on deposit with the bankers, so that when I returned I would have received it back with interest.

"So take the bag of gold from him and give it to the one who has ten bags. For whoever has will be given more, and they will have an abundance. Whoever does not have, even what they have will be taken from them. And throw that worthless servant outside, into the darkness, where there will be weeping and gnashing of teeth."

This law is applicable to the management of your oil. Have you been a good manager of your oil, pressing it, educating it, using it to its fullest potential? If not, why would the owner trust you with more; exposure, clients and connections? In the book *Outliers*, author Malcolm Gladwell says that it takes roughly ten thousand hours of practice to achieve mastery in a field. If you're asking the owner to give you more but you're not taking the time to perfect what you have, why would God entrust you with more? This is what the law is saying—focus on what you have and really take care of it, so I can bless you abundantly. When you read that it takes "10,000 hours to achieve mastery" that sounds like a chaser's approach not a runner's.

The Law of Loss, once it is recognized as the law that governs your potential, has a tremendously great benefit to the management of the business. It isn't yours, it's God's - if knowing that how would you treat the clients? Treat the staff? Also, will you be honorable and follow the laws? It would be difficult to run a company poorly if you're treating it with a high regard that it belongs to God.

Kingdom Position

The Kingdom of business needs you in it, you must occupy the culture of business with your influence and your idea. Jeff Bezos is the richest man in the world now and Amazon has grown the ecommerce market tremendously, also has impacted retail and consumer behavior - even grocery stores deliver. This is the purpose of God for the ministry of entrepreneurship and business leadership, God is no respecter of man. You may currently rent a booth at a barbershop or own one truck with the desire to own a logistics company. We all start somewhere, get committed, occupy until He comes, and make disciples out of Nations.

Remember, God told Adam to "be fruitful and multiply," which is "bring forth and excel" then God gave Adam more instructions, "have dominion and subdue," meaning "prevail against and bring into subjection" all things you have access to. In other words, "I've given you all you need to be successful, prevail against the weeds and things you don't understand, bring those into your order also. Once you bring forth your passion, use the tools I've given you, you will excel." Read that part again and highlight it! You can create wealth and impact culture once you learn to become yourself, access is granted to originals not copies.

God placed each one of us, like He placed Adam, around all we already need, I understand, for some, that it is easy to look around and feel uninspired. Your living conditions aren't what you dreamed about - mines weren't either. I encourage you to identify your passion and go to beauty from ashes because you cannot be fired, evicted or repossessed from your oil.

What made the widow's story fitting for this book was the process she went through. Process has become my favorite word in every language because it is an inevitable aspect of life. It is unavoidable, you're going to go through a process the easy way or the hard way. Be mindful of quick promotion, process is part of the beauty of entrepreneurship and it's entirely up to you whether you learn through it. See the widow didn't recognize her anointing yet she was willing to hear from someone who could guide her. She submitted to instruction and worked hard, without question. Entrepreneurship is a process that requires you to approach every day with the end goal in mind, there must be commitment and persistence to get to your desired destination. There will be moments where you get frustrated, it happens to all, but you must believe enough to not abandon.

Your approach to direction and your ability to be where you're at in life today effectively equips you to prosper tomorrow. Did you know that the way you view something (whether obstacle or opportunity) determines how it will impact your walk? I've stopped asking God why and replaced it with "thanks" or a simple question such as "what this is meant to teach me?" I've switched my view on situations according to where my heart showed me I was heading, so everything along the way prepares me for a part of the story at large.

Entrepreneurship requires love, passion and gratitude. Approach every moment with passion and victory because dominion and access are birthrights, you were born equipped to thrive, but you must know who you are.

Even if you have a day job, work your oil afterwards - build a strong side hustle or find a job that allows you to use your oil and pays you to learn how to press your oil better. I encourage you to tap into your potential. The goal will be to build until you no longer must manage, to me self-employment and entrepreneurship are two different things. Self-employment is working extra hard, becoming the manager, tech guru, janitor, assistant manager, chef and greeter. Entrepreneurship is different, although you will still be involved in the day to day operations and management of your company from an executive level, all the roles you were filling while being self-employed are now occupied by others.

You'll start off as self-employed (everyone does) but your passion will drive your business and your anointing will mature to entrepreneur because you're empowered and commissioned to thrive. I want you to strive to thrive.

Sweat Equity

Have you ever heard of the term *sweat equity*? Sweat equity is a necessary component to entrepreneurship, it's the labor no one sees and the failures you've overcome. Defined as the "contribution to a project or enterprise in the form of effort and toil." Sweat equity is your non-monetary contribution and is as valuable as cash equity. The bible says it this way in James 2:17 NIV "In the same way, faith by itself, if it is not accompanied by action, is dead." This is what people miss often, the hustle is just as important as the dollar. I know entrepreneurs that had nothing but drive and made million-dollar companies with very little startup capital. Sweat equity no one can take away from you.

I worked at a national chain restaurant for about 10 years and played various roles in the establishment from busboy to server, but I was most happy as a chef because I was able to take my passion for cooking and apply learning to it. Shortly after my time there, seeing a need, I said to myself "there currently isn't representation of Latino culture in the quick service industry besides Mexican food, California burritos or Tex-Mex cuisine, I want to introduce Panamanian street foods in a quick service concept." I graduated from Eastern Michigan University then quit the restaurant to get a job at a financial institution. Vowing to myself, never to work in the restaurant industry again until I returned as an owner.

Several years later, while doing well at the bank - growing and being promoted, hitting bonuses, etc, the feeling to create, market and sell this

Panamanian street food came back. I would say to myself, "I thought I moved on, I'm doing well now; just purchased a home, a new car, got married, child on the way - I don't want to cook anymore, I want to be a leader at this bank." Yet the fire grew and grew, my wife and I started cooking and selling lunches to our colleagues, staying up late and selling lunches to a third-shift auto plant, had church members and friends ordering lunches for themselves and their coworkers, all of this is fanning the flame. I studied the cottage food laws in Michigan (to the best of my understanding) and moved forward. One year and one month after a promotion, four months after purchasing my first home and new car, three months after getting married, and 2 months after finding out my wife was pregnant, October 31, 2012 was my last day at the bank and November 1, 2012 was my first day as a full-time entrepreneur.

We started cooking at home, myself, my wife and a friend. I would pass out fliers, take orders then deliver. We had our friend getting orders from an auto plant then we had a friend getting orders from a call center. We had no license and a home kitchen and started making Italian food because that was my background, then we fused Mexican food with the Italian because to say "try the Carimañola" got met with questions (this is before I learned what a target market was). We evolved in phases with three different menus and three different logos. My pregnant wife just slaying away in our kitchen. The little money would buy our food and pay our 1 staff member. Anything left over would cover bills (they were piling in and often late).

My credit took a significant nosedive, our savings dried out and I would cry myself to sleep but my son was on the way and I had to make this happen, I was too deep in! At this point, my family started helping us pay bills. Our car was almost repossessed (several times), home almost foreclosed, I had no money, just belief in myself and sweat equity. "Here's what we'll do" I'd tell my wife, "sell some tamales and tres leche cakes make some money, set aside tithe and some for reinvesting, pay a little on the gas and electric, so the lights won't cut off, put a little down on the transportation and shelter so our car won't get repossessed and mortgage won't foreclose. Buy some groceries so we don't go hungry." I was going through it, but God never turned on me, and my wife never made me feel inadequate. It hardly is glamorous initially (if ever for some), I was in a season of transitioning from runner to chaser and it pained me to ask for help even while drowning.

I'm convinced that if there is an unwavering passion behind your vision, a 'this must happen' belief will eventually alter all circumstances; mediocrity and greatness cannot walk hand and hand, at some point one must overcome.

When I quit my job, I told the leadership "Don't let me come back," In response, they asked, "Are you sure?" and I would say "Yes, 100%!" I had no idea what I would be embarking on, but I knew it would cause me to abandon my comfort zone. I knew I had to put work in beyond the kitchen and that was worth it for me. Eventually, you'll have to get comfortable with being uncomfortable and flexible enough to stretch yourself. You can't compromise effort and budget drive. There must be a willingness to pour everything into your goal. For the widow, going to get the bottles, pouring and packaging the oil, setting them aside (counting inventory), and speaking with Elisha all constituted as sweat equity. These steps that no one saw created the opportunity for her to "go, sell, pay your debts, and live off the rest—you and your sons."

Leave Earth Better, Infiltrate the Culture

Entrepreneurs create as much change as politicians. As an entrepreneur, you stimulate economy, create opportunity and challenge unemployment. I decided a long time ago that the ideas given to me by God must get out. I can't keep them housed in or I'll have a break down. Also, I can't keep them caged in because I'll miss out on the promise which belongs to me and by keeping them in, I'm mismanaging my own life. I concluded that these ideas may offend some, encourage most, and employee many.

These ideas are my anointing and the one thing God truly requires of me is to give them back to him, I do that by releasing them out of my heart and mind. Our journeys aren't going to be exactly the same, I pray that you find your anointing because it is a disservice to the Holy Spirit to live a life of untapped potential, feeding your family and influencing others by being someone else. I get really bothered when I see my friends (or associates) being someone else. I know the feeling all too well as for a long time I was everything but what God called me to be. I was what the pastor wanted, what I saw on TV, what I thought my family wanted. Not until I inquired of the Lord did I realize that the only real way to bless my children was to be who God called me to be.

In the Bible, the Earth and the World don't have the same meaning. *Earth* is the dirt, the actual Earth and all in it. While the *World* refers to the systems of the Earth such as banking, business, hospitality, healthcare and pharmacy, technology, and music. You can impact both—use your anointing to increase your successes with your gift, this is how you make the Earth itself better. You will be ridiculed for dreams, though they be anointed by God. You will be criticized for your faith, but you should rather be ridiculed than to look back and feel unaccomplished.

You're a millennial entrepreneur with a purpose and we're waiting for you to sell your oil!

Lesson 10: Your gift is supposed to serve others. Once you've perfected your gift, you will then be commanded to serve others according to 1 Peter 4:10 NLT

10a: The moment you choose to let your gift go to waste, you'll be the person harming instead of serving the world.

A LETTER FROM THE AUTHOR

Your oil is like the treasure in those old pirate books we read as kids. It takes work to find it, but once uncovered it's yours to do with as you desire. Keep your focus locked on winning. You cannot afford to be preoccupied with who is doing what, their Instagram postings, or the hype. Instead become occupied with pressing forward towards the mark which is the treasure, the oil!

I want to ask you to repeat the following prayer with me. Highlight it and return to it in a year's time as a way to say, "I made this decision one year ago today, by faith, and God has done so much in my business, family, and relationships since I've taken this leap of faith."

The prayer is simple, by faith, you say:

"Heavenly Father, I know that I've made mistakes and have fallen short. I also know that I have mismanaged relationships, money, and opportunities. I accept that Jesus died for my errors and I receive the gift of your only Son to heal, restore, and reposition me on the path to my destiny in Christ. In Jesus name I pray. Amen."

God wants you to thrive, the first step is the prayer of salvation. Next, I want to encourage you to find a Bible based church that preaches the Kingdom of God and its power. You will be transformed by the renewing of your mind because faith comes by hearing.

I'm excited to see what God is going to do in your life and in your business—a lot can change in one year *by faith*!

Remember, the world is waiting on you! Remove the words "can't" and "impossible" from your mouths, these are lies we tell ourselves when we don't want to give it our all! Find your oil, press you oil, influence the culture, and point to Christ millennial entrepreneur!

Odell Palacio

PERMISSIONS

Permission to quote and use language from the Amplified Bible granted by The Lockman Foundation.

Permission to quote and use language from the New Living Translation Bible granted by Tyndale House Foundation.

Permission to quote and use language from the New King James Version, New International Version, and New International Reader's Version granted by Harper Collins.

Permission to quote and use language from the English Standard Version Bible granted by Crossway/Good News Publishing.

Permission to quote and use language from the Contemporary English Version Bible granted by the American Bible Society.

REFERENCES

Gladwell, Malcolm. *Outliers: The Story of Success.* Back Bay Books, Little, Brown and Company, 2013.

Mackay, Harvey. *Dig Your Well Before You're Thirsty: The Only Networking Book You'll Ever Need.* Currency/Doubleday, 1999.

Müller, Max. *Essentials of Inventory Management.* American Management Association, 2011.

BE THE FIRST TO RECEIVE

Free Inspirational Devotionals

WWW.DREAMYPSI.COM/YOUVERSION

FOLLOW ME *As I* FOLLOW CHRIST

04164458-00961557

Printed in the United States
By Bookmasters